D0821713

WICKED
Strategies

**HOW COMPANIES CONQUER COMPLEXITY
AND CONFOUND COMPETITORS**

WICKED
Strategies

HOW COMPANIES CONQUER COMPLEXITY AND CONFOUND COMPETITORS

JOHN C. CAMILLUS

UNIVERSITY OF TORONTO PRESS
Toronto Buffalo London

© John C. Camillus 2016
Rotman-UTP Publishing
University of Toronto Press
Toronto Buffalo London
www.utppublishing.com
Printed in Canada

ISBN 978-1-4426-5055-8

∞ Printed on acid-free, 100% post-consumer recycled paper
with vegetable-based inks.

Library and Archives Canada Cataloguing in Publication

Camillus, John C., author
Wicked Strategies : how companies conquer complexity and confound
competitors / John C. Camillus.

Includes bibliographical references and index.
ISBN 978-1-4426-5055-8 (bound)

1. Strategic planning. 2. Business planning. 3. Organizational change.
I. Title.

HD30.28.C35375 2016   658.4'012   C2016-901800-8

University of Toronto Press acknowledges the financial assistance to its
publishing program of the Canada Council for the Arts and the Ontario Arts
Council, an agency of the Government of Ontario.

Canada Council   Conseil des Arts
for the Arts   du Canada

ONTARIO ARTS COUNCIL
CONSEIL DES ARTS DE L'ONTARIO
an Ontario government agency
un organisme du gouvernement de l'Ontario

Funded by the   Financé par le
Government   gouvernement
of Canada   du Canada

Canadä

Contents

Figures and Tables

Figures

Tables

Preface

In business, some problems are easy, some problems are hard, and some problems are so complex, so intractable, and so threatening to organizations – or entire industries – that they are best described as "wicked." These problems resist easy interpretation or understanding; they pose questions which seem, to observers, to be unsolvable; and, they render traditional analytical tools of strategy virtually impotent, requiring new approaches to analysis. To the fascination and horror of managers, wicked scenarios, and the consequent wicked strategy problems that follow in their wake, are becoming increasingly commonplace.

The hallmark of a wicked situation is a rapidly transforming business environment in which established models of profitability and success are undergoing unpredictable and sea changes. To managers facing a wicked problem, it can feel as if the ground is shifting under their feet so quickly that no one knows what will happen next; all that is clear is that traditional solutions no longer work in the new environment. The wicked scenario is made more difficult because the perceived problem itself keeps changing as different solutions are considered.

Wicked problems were first recognized in the public policy arena as an entirely different class of problems, requiring entirely new problem solving approaches. In the United States, immigration issues, terrorism, religious fundamentalism, racism, and gun violence are such problems. In India, corruption, religious fundamentalism, communal violence, violence against women, and rural poverty are equally daunting issues that have so far resisted solution. They are caused by a multiplicity of interrelated factors, are viewed differently by different parties, have no apparent solution, and mutate as different "solutions" are considered. In our technology age, wicked problems are a fact of life when designing and building large-scale information systems. The debacle that was the rollout of the "healthcare.gov" website supporting the Affordable Care Act in the United States is not an atypical experience with large-scale information systems.

Over the years, I have observed the increasing frequency of the occurrence of wicked problems faced by managers in organizations through both my consulting and my research. In my 2008 *Harvard Business Review* article titled "Strategy as a Wicked Problem," I wrote about how managers can identify and more effectively respond to wicked problems in the arena of competitive strategy. The article excited a huge response from academics, consultants, and managers. Bayer and PPG were among the companies that made the article required reading for senior managers.

Encouraged by the response to the article, I have written this book to provide an updated, comprehensive, and detailed "how-to manual" for identifying, responding to, and even profiting from wicked problems. This book details the significant forces that underlie the increasing frequency with which wicked problems are encountered. And, as in certain martial arts, it shows you how to skillfully and resolutely turn these threatening forces to your advantage in handling wicked problems.

What the book offers are what millennials would call "wicked cool" approaches to manage wicked problems in the strategic management of organizations – what we will refer to more succinctly as

"Wicked Strategies." The Wicked Strategies presented in the book are drawn from the hundreds of organizations for which I have consulted. I have also researched Wicked Strategies in depth as part of five global benchmarking studies in which I have been involved. Wicked Strategies are one of the major foci of the case studies I have developed for a global, ongoing, permanently funded project called the Business of Humanity®. Based on the experiences of the organizations that were studied, I am confident that Wicked Strategies will work for you. But, just to increase your confidence, I have included a soupçon of theory and have also used a couple of widely known strategy frameworks to support the Wicked Strategies that are described.

The Wicked Strategies approach I present is occasionally counterintuitive, is substantially unconventional, and is, I hope, inspirational. Wicked Strategies prepare firms and managers to prevail over paradoxes, and to create and profitably exploit disruptions. Wicked Strategies are designed to enable firms to achieve two apparently conflicting, yet utterly necessary goals. Wicked Strategies ensure economic sustainability by positioning a firm to (1) aggressively seek to enhance the competitive advantage of their existing businesses, while at the same time (2) resolutely transform to make the existing businesses obsolete before the context or competition does it to them.

The secret to achieving these apparently conflicting goals is an evocative and enduring strategy construct, a dynamic and ambidextrous organizational structure, and an innovative and visionary set of analytical processes that form a management system that creates and deploys Wicked Strategies.

Throughout the book I have striven to keep both explanations and recommendations simple. When three forces can capture and illustrate the impact of a host of factors, and when responding to these three forces leads to managerial frameworks and responses that effectively address and respond to the host of factors, I have opted to share my identification of the three forces rather than offer a comprehensive and impressive but confusing list of possible factors. When three constructs can create a framework that can respond effectively to wicked problems in general, I opt to limit my recommendations to these three rather than offer a scholarly inventory of constructs from which you have to choose. In seeking focus and simplicity, I relied on my experience and my interpretation of academic research. You may see this as a limitation of the book or as a strength.

My education and training at the three amazing and wonderful institutions that I had the extreme good fortune to attend – Harvard Business School for my doctorate, the Indian Institute of Management, Ahmedabad, for my master's in management, and the Indian Institute of Technology, Madras, for my bachelor's in mechanical engineering – taught me that, as a professional, the most important question to ask is, "So, how does this understanding affect what we should be doing differently at 9:00 a.m. on Monday morning?" It is the question I have asked the thousands of graduate students and practicing managers whom I have taught, the scores of clients for whom I have consulted on four continents, and the dozens of academic colleagues and experts with whom I have interacted. It is this question, in the context of wicked problems, which this book seeks to answer.

It is my intent and hope that the Wicked (cool) Strategies that this book shows you how to develop and implement will increase your ability and confidence to handle the daunting challenges posed by Wicked (evil) Problems.

If you have any thoughts or suggestions on how to improve these Wicked Strategies, please drop me a note at john.camillus@ induscommons.com. I will make the best of these comments and suggestions available to you and your fellow readers at www. induscommons.com.

John Camillus
Pittsburgh, 2015

Acknowledgments

This book would not have been written but for the unfailing help and constant encouragement of my wife Ruth, whose invaluable support began with the writing of my doctoral dissertation decades ago, and has continued unabated over the years. My two sons, who count MBAs among their several degrees, put their education and work experience to use and contributed greatly to the book. Joseph gently steered me away from my inclination towards excessive detail and onerous theoretical expositions. He motivated and helped me to rethink the overly complex model with which I started. He led me to identify and focus on the necessary and sufficient essentials of the Feed-Forward Framework that is offered in the book. Conversations with Michael significantly helped me develop and refine the logic underlying the model. Also, he identified, researched, and fleshed out many of the real-world examples that I employ.

As this may be one of the last books I will write, I think it is time for me to acknowledge my brother Dr Joseph Camillus's invisible but crucial impact on my career. He prepared me to get into and graduate with distinction from the extremely selective Indian Institute of Technology, Madras, and Indian Institute of Management, Ahmedabad (IIMA). He prompted me to choose Harvard over a less daunting alternative, and gave me the emotional support and indispensable advice that, as a little traveled and inexperienced youth, I needed to master the challenge of this great university.

Four professors had a hand in transforming me from an operations jock into a researcher and designer of strategic planning and management control systems – Professors S.K. Bhattacharyya and Prafull Anubhai of IIMA, and Professors John Dearden and Richard Vancil of Harvard. I owe them an inestimable debt of gratitude.

My heartfelt thanks to Jennifer DiDomenico, acquisitions editor of the University of Toronto Press, who convinced me of the advantages of going with her pioneering and prestigious press. She thoughtfully shepherded the manuscript through the rigorous review process of an academic publisher, and carefully vetted the final draft, as she said, "with a fine-toothed comb."

Finally, the thousands of students – MBA, doctoral, and executive – who motivated and challenged me, and asked the beautiful questions that educated me, have left their imprint on this book. And I cannot adequately thank the hundreds of organizations who generously "trusted but verified" my consulting advice, affirmed my thinking, and gave me the confidence that this book may be worthwhile writing and could be of value and help to managers faced with wicked problems.

WICKED
Strategies

HOW COMPANIES CONQUER COMPLEXITY
AND CONFOUND COMPETITORS

PART 1

UNDERSTANDING WICKED PROBLEMS AND WICKED STRATEGIES

Wicked Problems and Wicked Strategies: Recognizing and Responding to the Challenge

The future is uncertain ... but this uncertainty is at the very heart of human creativity.

Ilya Prigogine

Complexity and uncertainty are the two reasons why management and managers are needed. These are the two fundamental challenges that stand between managers and the economic viability of their organizations. In today's business environment, complexity and uncertainty are not implicit or hidden. They stare managers in the face and provoke paralysis in decision making. While there are many forces that fuel uncertainty and complexity, in my experience, three forces in particular – globalization, disruptive innovations, and stakeholder demands – are taking these challenges to never-before-seen levels of difficulty, a level that has earned the sobriquet "wicked."

Traditionally, managers have dealt with complexity by trying to break the problem down into smaller problems. But there are degrees and variations of complexity that are not readily amenable to deconstruction. And if the application of each small solution changes the underlying nature of the other small problems, it becomes impossible to solve complex problems piece by piece.

Techniques that managers employ to deal with uncertainty and risk, such as contingency planning, focus on coping with volatility.

But uncertainty comes in different forms than simple volatility – there could be entirely different alternative futures and, furthermore, these futures could be clouded by ambiguity.[1] When these extreme variations of uncertainty and complexity interact, wickedness results, as illustrated in figure 1.1.

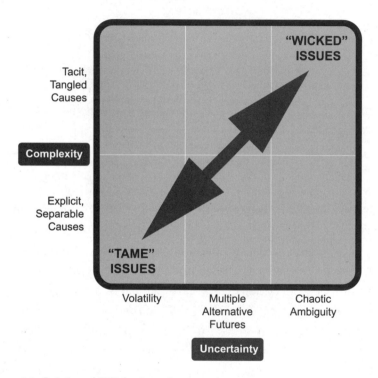

Figure 1.1 Origins of "Wickedness"

A wicked problem has many tangled causes, rather than a single, obvious cause. It often appears unprecedented, and its appearance is unpredictable, something "no one" has anticipated. The problem affects multiple parties, often with conflicting interests, and has no single, demonstrably correct answer. Rather than appearing fixed, a wicked problem morphs constantly. Obeying something akin to the laws of quantum physics, where the very act of observation affects the state of the phenomenon, the underlying nature of a wicked problem changes depending on the solution under consideration. Virtually all of these factors mean that traditional strategic planning processes simply cannot cope with wicked problems. Widely used strategic planning techniques such as five-forces analysis and value-chain analysis, as conventionally employed, are not useful in these situations. Strategic planning must transform in response to a world that is more complex and uncertain, more wicked. Wicked strategic issues often render the future unknowable; they fracture industry boundaries, disrupt technologies, and create discontinuities.

Horst W.J. Rittel and Melvin M. Webber, professors of design and urban planning at the University of California at Berkeley, first described wicked problems in a 1973 article in *Policy Sciences* magazine. They identified ten characteristics of wicked problems. Over the years, I have whittled these ten criteria down to a more manageable but equally powerful five. These five defining characteristics of wicked problems, which render traditional problem-solving approaches impotent, are:

1 The perceived "problem" is unusual and substantially without precedent.
2 There are multiple, significant stakeholders with conflicting values and priorities who are affected by the perceived problem or responses to the problem.
3 There are many apparent causes of the problem and they are inextricably tangled.
4 It is impossible to be sure when you have the correct or best solution; there is a "no stopping" rule.
5 The understanding of what the "problem" is changes when reviewed in the context of alternative proposed solutions.

Problems possessing these characteristics are far from amenable to solution by traditional methods. Traditional methods need a clear and accepted definition of the problem, which is hard to come by when the problem is unprecedented, and different solutions interact with and affect the problem. Well-defined alternative solutions to the problem need to be generated, which is difficult when the problem is unusual and unprecedented, and becomes impossible when each solution being considered changes the perception of the problem. Also, there has to be an accepted criterion or criteria that can be applied to evaluate the alternatives, which is problematic when different stakeholders have different priorities and goals.

The challenges posed by wicked *strategic* issues, similarly, simply overwhelm conventional strategy formulation processes. Classic strategy processes assume that:

- The future is predictable, if enough effort and the right techniques are employed.

    How is that possible when the issue is unprecedented and disruptive?

- Competitors in the same "industry" are the major challenge and outwitting them is the goal.

    But industries today are at risk of being disrupted, transformed, converged, disintermediated, and obsoleted. Competition from unexpected global sources is now commonplace, and rethinking the industry definition is necessary but has wicked undertones.

- Defining the strategic issue with clarity is the first step, leading to testing well-defined solutions against existing and objective criteria to select the best response.

    This is the traditional problem-solving approach, which we know is helpless in the face of wickedness.

So we now know what the challenge is.

Acknowledging the existence of and recognizing the nature of wicked problems is not enough. We need to accept and overcome the challenges that they pose. This book offers "Wicked Strategies" as the answer to wicked problems. These Wicked Strategies have been identified and developed based on what I have observed inventive organizations to be doing and my resulting understanding of how companies can cope with and, indeed, profit from the ubiquitous forces that breed wicked problems.

The Seeds of Wicked Problems

The Wicked Strategies that we will develop are designed to work by dealing with wicked problems at their source, addressing the forces that engender the challenges that interact to create wicked problems. There are driving forces in the business environment that are both ubiquitous and potent. While there are a host of such factors, the perspective adopted here is to identify significant forces that, in concert, offer an evocative and workable understanding of reality – much like Niels Bohr's willingness to accept a mathematical model that offered a manageable representation of reality, as opposed to Albert Einstein's search for "truth."[2] In adopting this perspective, there are three driving forces that, in my experience, dominate and substantially encapsulate or reflect the other factors.

Three Mega-Forces

The inevitability of intensifying globalization. Even organizations that make a deliberate choice to limit the geographic scope of their target markets will inevitably encounter issues of globalization because of the ever-increasing importance of global sourcing, global competition, global standards, global quality expectations, global partnerships, and global financing. Moreover, there is the pull of emerging markets[3] with estimates of untapped purchasing power in the trillions of dollars.

The increasing incidence and importance of innovation. Innovation is essential in order to respond to or evade competitive developments, to anticipate customer expectations, to cope with change, to support growth, and to enable sustainability. The maturity of markets in developed countries and the relatively slow growth rate in these markets place a premium on innovation by firms as an accelerant. In the emerging economies, too, innovation is what enables firms to catch up with or leapfrog competitors in the developed economies.

The growing imperative and inspirational impact of diverse stakeholders who merit and demand shared value. Milton Friedman's singular focus on shareholder value[4] is increasingly seen as leading managers to make decisions that may be suboptimal and perhaps even damaging to the bottom line. Economic value and societal good are argued by gurus of strategic thinking to be synergistic.[5] Engaging a variety of stakeholders – employees, the community, customers, government, creditors, social activists – and responding thoughtfully to their perceived interests is expected to enhance economic and shareholder value, possibly in the short run and certainly in the long run. As a consequence, there is a growing recognition that shared value can and should inform and inspire the raison d'être of firms.

These three pervasive influences on the business environment are truly mega-forces. They can have a powerful impact on business strategies. *Globalization* brings complexity and uncertainty; *innovation* creates new realities, unprecedented situations, and conflict among stakeholders who are affected by the resulting changes; and *shared value* recognizes multiple and conflicting priorities and goals among those who have a stake in or are affected by the organization. While they are significant, they can be addressed individually by traditional approaches to strategy formulation. When they interact, however, the resulting complex challenges are what create wicked problems that render traditional approaches impotent.

The Strategic Challenges

The interactions of the three mega-forces create the climate in which wicked problems flourish. The interactions between the mega-forces give rise to the existential challenges of disruptive technologies, conflicted stakeholders, and unknowable futures.

First, the interactions between globalization and innovation tend to create *disruptive technologies*. Globalization is strongly colored by the accelerating significance of emerging economies and the multi-trillion-dollar purchasing capacity of the "bottom of the pyramid."[6] Meeting the very different needs of low-income customers demands fundamental changes in the business model – in product design and packaging, the application of frugal engineering to lower costs, new pricing, new distribution channels, different promotion practices, and focused R&D. Hart and Christensen[7] argue persuasively that addressing the needs of the bottom of the pyramid will require and result in the development of *disruptive technologies*.

Second, innovation and shared value interact to create *conflicted stake-holders*.[8] Innovation can enable and even require changes in the business model. New business models will generate value in novel ways, changing the relevance and importance of existing stakeholders, and requiring a fresh and different understanding of how the value will be shared. *Conflict between stakeholders* is likely to happen as a result.

Third, the interaction between shared value and globalization generates unpredictable and perhaps *unknowable futures*.[9] The reason is that shared value engages multiple stakeholders with different priorities. Globalization is characterized by extreme complexity and uncertainty. Mixing the two – stakeholders with conflicting goals and the backdrop of extreme complexity and uncertainty – creates unpredictable, alternative *futures that may be truly unknowable*.

At the center of these three interactions – the incendiary mixture of disruptive technologies, conflicted stakeholders, and an unknowable future – is the incubator in which wicked problems are created.[10] This is the decision space in which Wicked Strategies are needed, and where the hidden opportunity exists for astute strategists to create competitive advantage. (See figure 1.2.)

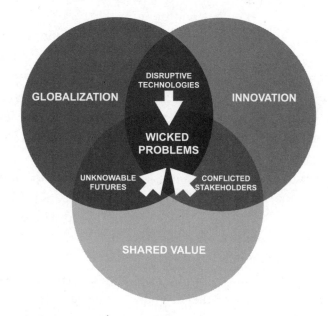

Figure 1.2 The Interactions of the Mega-Forces

Crafting the Framework for Developing Wicked Strategies

With this understanding of how wicked problems may emerge, we now have the foundation needed to build effective Wicked Strategies. In presenting the logic and developing a framework for creating and implementing Wicked Strategies, I have employed a corollary of Occam's Razor. I have focused on offering the most straightforward, simple, and useful approach. At each stage in the process I have sought to identify the smallest number of elements that can provide for a comprehensive and effective response to wicked problems. This effort has resulted fortuitously, but not by intent, in three elements at each stage in the process. Three elements are easy to comprehend, remember, and act upon. The framework that results lends itself to ready understanding, setting the stage for effective implementation.

The first step in the process of developing the framework is to be aware of mega-forces in the environment that make transformative demands on business strategies. The three mega-forces that have been identified – *globalization*, *innovation*, and *shared value* – provide us with a simple but focused and illuminating basis for proceeding to the second step.

The second step is to recognize the strategic challenges – *disruptive technologies*, *conflicted stakeholders*, and *unknowable futures* – created by the interactions of these mega-forces. These strategic challenges create the context in which wicked problems – ill-defined, unprecedented, constantly morphing problems with no evident solutions, which impact demanding and diverse stakeholders – breed. Addressing these challenges would respond to wicked problems at their source and possibly even pre-empt them. So, in this step, responses to each of the three challenges are proposed. This is done in chapters 2 through 4.

The third step is to aggregate and review the responses developed to each of the strategic challenges, identify and eliminate redundancies, and then cluster related responses together. This is done in chapter 5. Three clusters emerge – labeled *identity*, *feed-forward*, and *modular structure* – which form the components of a *feed-forward framework* designed to develop Wicked Strategies. Each of these clusters is discussed in chapters 6 through 8.

The fourth and final step is to employ the feed-forward framework to develop Wicked Strategies that address the strategic challenges by metamorphosing them into opportunities. Wicked Strategies embrace disruptive technologies to create *innovative business models,* engage conflicted stakeholders to *co-create value,* and resolve and master unknowable futures through *feed-forward* processes. (See figure 1.3.) Developing the feed-forward framework and demonstrating its application to create Wicked Strategies is the focus of chapters 9 and 10.

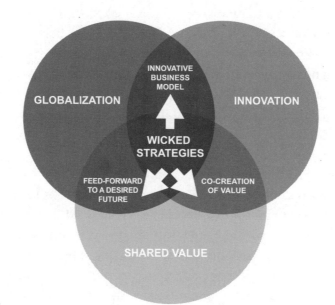

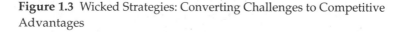

Figure 1.3 Wicked Strategies: Converting Challenges to Competitive Advantages

The design logic leading from the recognition of transformative environmental *mega-forces* to the *feed-forward framework* for developing and deploying *Wicked Strategies* is diagrammed in figure 1.4.

The feed-forward framework is designed to achieve the exquisite alchemy of transmuting strategic challenges into competitive advantage and added value. What the Feed-Forward Framework is intended to create is a firm that embraces change and transformation, yet maintains an enduring and proud identity; a firm that

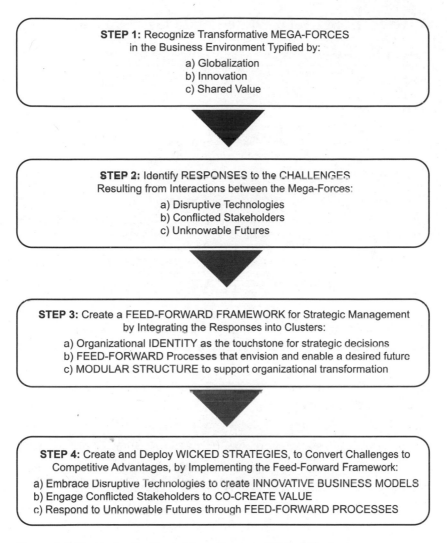

STEP 1: Recognize Transformative MEGA-FORCES
in the Business Environment Typified by:
a) Globalization
b) Innovation
c) Shared Value

STEP 2: Identify RESPONSES to the CHALLENGES
Resulting from Interactions between the Mega-Forces:
a) Disruptive Technologies
b) Conflicted Stakeholders
c) Unknowable Futures

STEP 3: Create a FEED-FORWARD FRAMEWORK for Strategic Management
by Integrating the Responses into Clusters:
a) Organizational IDENTITY as the touchstone for strategic decisions
b) FEED-FORWARD Processes that envision and enable a desired future
c) MODULAR STRUCTURE to support organizational transformation

STEP 4: Create and Deploy WICKED STRATEGIES, to Convert Challenges to
Competitive Advantages, by Implementing the Feed-Forward Framework:
a) Embrace Disruptive Technologies to create INNOVATIVE BUSINESS MODELS
b) Engage Conflicted Stakeholders to CO-CREATE VALUE
c) Respond to Unknowable Futures through FEED-FORWARD PROCESSES

Figure 1.4 Design Logic: From Mega-Forces to Wicked Strategies

prizes its employees and engages its stakeholders as the creators of societal benefit and economic value for its shareholders; and a firm that unflinchingly faces and, indeed, exploits an unknowable future.

Differences Between Wicked and Classic Strategies

Table 1.1 Characteristics of "Wicked" and "Classic" Strategies

Characteristic	Wicked	Classic Competitive
Dominant management mindset	Learn from the future *Feed-forward*	Learn from the past *Feedback*
Response to external disruptive change	Exploit opportunity for competitive advantage *Create / embrace*	Resist and double-down on sustaining innovation *Resist*
Orientation towards organizational transformation	Stimulate and support *Continuous*	Transform only as a survival response *Episodic*
Sustainability of strategy	Organizational identity transcends external disruptions and organizational transformations *Intrinsically enduring*	Competitive strategy threatened by disruptive external developments and organizational transformation *Inherently obsolescent*

Wicked Strategies differ from classic strategies in fundamental ways. For instance, classic strategies endeavor to grow a business by seeking and selecting adjacencies.[11] The underlying rationale is to use existing competencies in the search for growth outside the core. The concept of a core competency,[12] often relating to a technology or a business process, guides the identification of adjacencies. Wicked Strategies, by contrast, because they are responsive to disruptions, do not have the luxury of restricting growth to adjacencies. A core competency in the context of Wicked Strategies would be the ability to constantly develop and add to the existing competencies of the organization. Classic strategic analysis attempts to predict and respond to an expected future. Wicked Strategies recognize the futility of attempting predictions in the face of extreme uncertainty and complexity and attempt to create a desired future, reaching out to new arenas that can be cultivated by a dynamic array of inter-related competencies.

The distinction between the classic strategies that most organizations formulate and implement today and the Wicked Strategies that are proposed here are summarized in table 1.1.

To provide a preliminary taste of what a Wicked Strategy might be, let's look at an example from a 30,000-foot vantage point. For instance, the difference between a Classic approach and a Wicked-Strategies approach to expanding into fast-growing, large, emerging economies, such as Brazil, China, and India, is fundamental. The two approaches are diagrammed in figure 1.5.

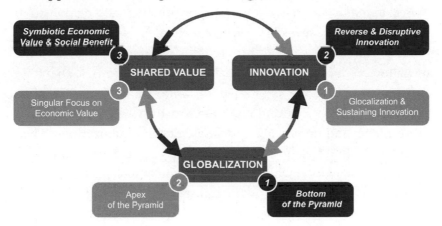

Figure 1.5 Examples of Classic and Wicked Strategies

Classic strategies would tend to:

1 "glocalize" existing products by marginally modifying existing products in developed economies for the emerging markets, and emphasizing sustaining innovations; then
2 target the small, upper-income segments – the apex of the pyramid – in emerging markets; and
3 focus primarily, if not solely, on economic value added.

A Wicked Strategy, in contrast, would:

1 focus on the special needs of the vast populations at the bottom of the pyramid and the tens of millions of people entering the middle class in emerging economies to identify novel value propositions;

2 generate relevant disruptive technologies, through customer insight[13] and frugal engineering,[14] to meet the needs and price-point expectations of low-income customers; and

3 seek the potential synergy, or the mutual enhancement, of economic value and social benefit.

In chapters 2, 3, and 4, we will explore and develop responses to the strategic challenges of disruptive technologies, conflicted stakeholders, and unknowable futures that result from interactions of the mega-forces. By analyzing and clustering these responses, chapter 5 develops the components of a feed-forward framework – identity, feed-forward processes, and modular structure – which are needed to formulate and deploy Wicked Strategies in organizations. Then chapters 6, 7, and 8 elaborate on each of the components of the feed-forward framework. Finally, chapter 9 symbiotically integrates the components of the feed-forward framework, and chapter 10 concludes with a real-time demonstration of the use of the feed-forward framework to Walmart, one of the most significant corporations in the world.

CHAPTER 2

Disruptive Technologies: Origins and Opportunities

Every threat to the status quo is an opportunity in disguise.

Jay Samit

If we don't change direction soon, we'll end up where we're going.

Professor Irwin Corey

In the rolling cauldron that is the business environment today, three mega-forces are responsible for creating wicked problems in the business environment. *Globalization* brings complexity and uncertainty, *innovation* creates new and unfamiliar realities, unprecedented situations, and potential conflict, and, finally, *shared value* recognizes multiple stakeholders with conflicting priorities and goals. These three mega-forces are, of course, individually important, but it is their *interaction* that creates wicked problems and the compelling need for Wicked Strategies.

The interactions between *globalization* and *innovation* create the possibility of *disruptive technologies*. Christensen, Raynor, and McDonald[1] emphasize that disruptive innovations arise from addressing low-end markets or from the creation of entirely new markets. Globalization creates the context in which low-end markets are found and entirely new markets can be conceived.

The resulting disruptive innovations and related technologies in turn create the need and the opportunity for new business models. How this comes about and how the process can be managed is the focus of this chapter.

Occasionally the argument is made that sustaining innovations over time can create substantial change. This may seem to blur the distinction between disruptive innovation and sustaining innovation. However, there is a fundamental difference between sustaining and disruptive technologies and innovations that informs our discussion. Sustaining innovation addresses the needs of existing customers and improves existing products to better meet these perceived needs. Disruptive technologies and innovations, by contrast, create new markets that would otherwise not exist or be accessible by the firm.

FROM DISRUPTIVE TECHNOLOGIES TO INNOVATIVE BUSINESS MODELS

Globalization and *innovation* interact in significant and complex ways. Multinational companies are shifting their R&D investment and activities to the emerging and rapidly growing economies, particularly China and India. Moreover, the vast, vastly different and difficult to access markets in emerging economies require new business models – everything from redesigning products and services at much lower price points to employing novel distribution methods. The interaction of R&D with these markets creates a fertile field for technological innovation, spurred by the price-point pressures exerted by large, low-income populations. Let's now explore the dimensions of the interactions between globalization and innovation.

The data indicating the shift of corporate R&D investment to the BRIC (Brazil, Russia, India, and China) economies are dramatic and compelling. A 2006 study by Yves Doz of INSEAD and several others[2] found that companies located 50 percent more research sites in foreign countries than in their own countries of origin. At the time of the study, the investments of US firms in R&D in China and India were on the verge of exceeding the firms' investments in Western Europe.

This pronounced shift, to China and India in particular, is readily understood through the lens of traditional strategic analysis. Qualified and competent researchers are available in these countries at a fraction of the cost that would be incurred in the Triad (European Union, Japan, and the United States). And there is a less obvious but equally consequential reason for the shift: to position research assets in close proximity to the promising markets in the BRIC countries and other emerging economies.

According to Harvard Business School professor Clayton Christensen,[3] the guru of disruptive innovation, combining (1) the research, product development, manufacturing, and marketing functions of a Triad-based firm with (2) millions of potential customers in a BRIC location, who have relatively low income and different needs, can be expected to result in spontaneous combustion; in other words, the emergence of disruptive technologies, products, and related new business models.

The economic motivation, of course, is the $5 trillion (2005 international dollars)[4] to $13 trillion (the latter estimate employing 2004 Purchasing Power Parity)[5] of untapped purchasing power of the four billion people at the base of the pyramid. But it is impractical to tap into this immense reservoir of potential revenue and profits by offering the same products and services offered to customers at the apex of the pyramid. Indeed, price-point pressures are what trigger disruptive technologies and products. Christensen, writing about the "innovator's dilemma,"[6] points out that while classic strategies are well equipped to handle sustaining innovation, they are inherently ill-suited to respond effectively to disruptive innovation.

So, an important objective of Wicked Strategies would be to harness disruptive technologies to create value. We will explain how Wicked Strategies can be designed to create value from disruptive innovation in chapters 6 and 10.

Precisely how disruptive technologies emerge was explained[7] by Professor Ashok Jhunjhunwala of the Indian Institute of Technology, Madras, India's foremost engineering school. Jhunjhunwala's accomplishments have been internationally recognized and honored by the Government of India with the prestigious Padma Bhushan award. An expert in communications technology, Jhunjhunwala motivated a team of his computer and electrical engineering colleagues to join him in an ambitious venture to bring modern communication to rural India. At that time, in the early eighties, India had a population of approximately a billion people, but a minuscule ten million telephones, of which almost all were city-based landlines. Jhunjhunwala's visionary goal was to increase coverage to 100 million telephone lines, which would also be made accessible to the rural population.

His organization – which was incorporated under the name Tenet – found that it took more than advances in technology, no matter how technically brilliant, to be successful. They found that even dramatically lowering price points, while it did make the communication products and services more accessible, was also not enough. The pressure to lower costs did stimulate technological breakthroughs, but Jhunjhunwala found that the team's accomplishments and progress towards its goal were minimal until a eureka moment occurred.

Becoming One with the Customer

Jhunjhunwala, pondering the team's lack of progress, suddenly came to the conclusion that their singular focus on communications technology was holding them back. He realized that for the impoverished rural population, communications technology was of little interest in comparison to larger concerns. What rural Indians wanted and needed, he said, was "health, education and livelihood." This might seem to have been obvious from the start, but it is typical of companies to blithely assume that what they have to offer is what new customers want, especially if another higher-income group is receptive to it.

Jhunjhunwala's epiphany on the psychology of low-income customers led to several developments. His company fashioned innovative value propositions based on harnessing communications technology to provide, for example, programmed primary and secondary education, basic telemedicine services, and jobs for managers of local kiosks that would offer the telecommunication services. As Tenet expanded its operations, many outside businesses were positively affected. Companies were formed, investors were attracted, rural India benefited, and Jhunjhunwala ultimately received one of the highest honors from the Indian government for his technological, economic, and social contributions.

A typical business that emerged was a company involved in the development of efficient algorithms that compressed voice recordings into packets of data that were much smaller than what had previously been possible. This disruptive technology was motivated by the commitment to address the communication needs of the largely illiterate rural population. A form of e-mail communication between individuals who could not read and write was made possible by this development. It enabled the use of basic, slow, and cheap computers to efficiently record and communicate voice messages rather than written messages. This compression technology was extended to video, and one of Jhunjhunwala's companies was able to develop and build DSL routers that could, amazingly, send eleven movies simultaneously through the ancient, degraded copper wire that served the few telephones that existed in rural India.

It was abundantly evident, as Jhunjhunwala discovered, that disruptive technologies by themselves were not enough to bring about change, or to provide economic or social benefit. The value of disruptive technologies, he found, lies instead in their potential to offer new value propositions, enable supporting processes, and generate new profit models. Furthermore, to create effective value propositions, the needs of customers who are very different from the customers which companies are used to serving have to be insightfully divined and addressed. This is why locating research in emerging markets, enabling researchers and engineers to interact with and relate to these different customers, offers benefits that go far beyond cost savings.

There is a critically important lesson to be derived from Jhunjhunwala's experience at Tenet. To be successful, we must walk in the customers' shoes. The kiosk operators that Tenet set up in rural India were both part of the Tenet's operations and were staffed by the archetypical customer that Tenet was seeking to serve. The kiosk operators provided an understanding of customer needs that no outsider could possibly offer. They functioned as distributors and providers of Tenet's services and products; they served as test markets and sources of insights about Tenet's customers' needs; and they were the beneficiaries of Tenet's strategic commitment to providing livelihood opportunities.

Integrating Social Responsibility into the Business Model

There is a related heartwarming and motivational tale of a Wicked Strategy that I encountered in my research. It involves Arvind Limited, a global textile manufacturer based in India that reduced the incidence of cotton farmers committing suicide – a tragedy that is all too common in India.

The farmers who were most at risk worked on non-irrigated land, dependent on monsoon rains. They borrowed money to pay for expensive, genetically modified, pest-resistant seeds, and for fertilizers and pesticides. If successive monsoon rains failed to occur, the farmers were likely to be unable to pay back the money they borrowed, and their land would be forfeited to the moneylenders. With no ability to make an alternative living, farmers and their families often chose suicide to slow death by starvation.

Arvind, a public limited company, which began as a textile manufacturer, has a fourth-generation scion of the founding family as its CEO. Arvind's reputation for implementing leading management practices has made it the focus of several case studies that are discussed in management schools in India. Every generation of the family has been recognized for its commitment to social responsibility, a commitment that has seen a progression from personal giving, to corporate giving, to professionally managed philanthropic trusts funded by the company, to the current generation's innovative and surprisingly profitable incorporation of social responsibility into business models implemented by Arvind.

Motivated by their concern for the farmers, and by the company's and its major customers' (including Walmart and Patagonia) avowed commitment to environmental and social sustainability, Arvind's CEO and senior executives brainstormed a possible response to the farmers' precarious circumstances. The answer they came up with was to teach and enable the farmers to engage in organic cotton farming.

Organic farming, they believed, would get farmers out of the clutches of moneylenders because organic farming is fertilizer- and pesticide-free. Even the cost of cotton seed was significantly reduced because expensive genetically modified seeds were not employed. Arvind's project took enormous commitment, a great deal of courage, some creativity, and rigorous planning and analysis. A detailed business plan was developed. The company recruited 130 agronomists and embedded them in the villages to offer scientific counsel tailored to each farmer's small plot of land and fundamentally change traditional farming practices. Arvind also assumed control of the value chain surrounding the farmers' activities, eliminating avaricious and exploitative middlemen.

But in order to achieve this splendid success – and this is the point that warrants emphasis – Arvind's executives truly had to become one with the farmers. The son of the CEO, a Yale-educated, immensely advantaged fifth-generation scion of the founding family, spent time in the villages. The head of Arvind's agribusiness also lived in the villages. Through these experiences, they understood the hardships and challenges faced by the local population. It is impossible for anyone unfamiliar with rural India to understand the resolve it takes for someone used to middle-class levels of comfort, let alone a person of privilege, to endure the conditions of living in a poor village. Arvind took their efforts to understand the local population to extreme lengths.

Beyond helping farmers to protect their lives and livelihoods, Arvind also protected the environment, engaged diverse stakeholders, enhanced its competitive position and standing with major international customers, and added significantly to its coffers. The moral is that Arvind's leadership became one with the farmers and the resulting tale of disruption, increased economic value added, and social benefit is illuminating and inspirational.[8]

Arvind has committed to and replicated the practice of incorporating social responsibility into business models to create disruptions and innovatively enhance both economic value and social benefit. One of these innovative businesses is real estate development and housing for slum dwellers. Another involves teaching tailoring skills and providing safe and comfortable housing to economically and socially disadvantaged young women, to ease Arvind's entry into the Indian garmenting industry, which is challenged by highly restrictive labor laws.

Building an Array of Inter-related Competencies

The Arvind example also suggests an important concomitant of addressing or creating disruptive technologies and building innovative business models. In order to address the plight of poor cotton farmers, Arvind had to add agronomy to its existing inventory of competencies. In working with the cotton farmers, and in keeping with the organic practice of not using chemical fertilizers, Arvind introduced crop rotation practices in order to keep the land fertile. Pulses were introduced in the years when cotton was not grown and this led to Arvind getting involved in helping the farmers in its organic cotton growing program to sell food crops. Based on its competence in agronomy and its newly developed understanding of growing and selling food crops, Arvind proceeded to create an entirely new and profitable agribusiness division.

Similarly, based on its long history of working in urban slums, providing infrastructure, and health and education services, Arvind received incentives from the state government to build housing for the slums with which it had a history. This then led to planned investment in real estate development and construction.

Arvind used its new construction competence to build world-class, 10,000-person dormitories for girls from very low-income, highly disadvantaged rural communities, whom they trained to get into the garmenting business. The garmenting industry in India has been challenging because of punitive government regulations restricting layoffs of the labor force. However, by positioning its entry into garmenting as an "earn and learn program," providing training for otherwise unemployable young women, Arvind was able to reduce the potential liability that it would otherwise incur. At the same time, young women who otherwise faced a bleak future were taught skills in a safe environment. These skills gave the young women the potential to earn an independent livelihood and also made them more marriageable in the Indian context.

A similar pattern of evolving and adding to an array of related competencies can be observed in the context of the other companies and examples discussed in this chapter.

Accepting Unique and Unserved Customer Needs as the Driver

There are a few other lessons about innovative business models based on disruptive technologies that need to be recognized when developing Wicked Strategies. A comprehensive and powerful example from which important lessons can be drawn is that of General Electric. Jeffrey Immelt, GE's CEO, along with two academics, Vijay Govindarajan and Chris Trimble, recently wrote a fascinating and immensely instructive article[9] that provided a radical perspective on competitive strategy and the management system needed to support it. They described the experience of GE's medical systems business in developing major breakthroughs in the cost and functionality of electrocardiogram (ECG) and ultrasound machines when engineers and scientists were charged with developing machines that could be profitably sold at a price point targeting the low-income segments of the Chinese and Indian populations. The ECG machines developed in India were battery-powered, because the electric grid did not reach into every village. The machines had to be small enough to fit on the back of a bicycle, which was often the only viable mode of transportation in rural areas. The machines had to be simple enough to be operated with little training, and they had to have telemedicine capabilities that would enable doctors in distant locations to review the data and assess the patient's condition. And, of course, the machines had to be made at a fraction of the cost of the existing products that had been developed to serve the higher-income populations of more developed countries.

The fact that GE accomplished these goals reinforces two lessons that Professor Jhunjhunwala learned. First, that the technology must be driven by customer and contextual needs. Management should not assume that if the technology is improved and achieves engineering-oriented, higher-performance goals that competitive advantage and business success will inevitably follow. Marginal improvements in existing technologies are unlikely to give rise to breakthrough or disruptive products and business models. Disruptive technologies are ones that make existing technologies obsolete – as e-mail made faxes obsolete. However, existing technologies that are newly brought to bear to serve the specific unmet needs of a market can also create a competitive advantage – for example, replacing viewfinders on video cameras with LCD screens, or adding telemedicine capabilities to ECG machines.

One of the most amazing examples of using existing technologies in the medical imaging industry to create a revolutionary product, new benefits for humanity, and economic value for firms involves the computerized tomography (CT) scanner. Dr Godfrey Hounsfield, a researcher with EMI, used existing X-ray, computing, and display technologies to configure a brilliant, game-changing, Nobel Prize–winning product that revolutionized the practice of medicine.

Innovating across the Entire Value Chain

In each of the above examples, there is a related point of significance, and it is that disruptive technologies may not be necessary to create disruptive business models. Other elements of the value chain can access untapped economic value and strengthen competitive advantage in new markets. These elements could be as simple as new packaging or as complex as creating a distribution system that accesses remote customers and shares value with the customers and other stakeholders.

Innovation across the entire value chain can be promoted by engaging customers and other stakeholders in the creation of value. Richard Norman and Rafael Ramirez[10] describe a constellation of value created by "suppliers, business partners, allies, customers – work[ing] together to co-produce value."

Let's consider the example of Cavinkare, which began as a personal care startup called Chik India, and is now a highly successful FMCG manufacturer. The company started with an initial investment of less than $300 in 1983 and grew to a $250 million company by 2014. It got its start with the now-ubiquitous, single-use sachets of shampoo. These sachets were affordable for the hundreds of millions of customers earning less than $2 a day, who could not afford to buy a whole bottle of shampoo. A simple innovation in packaging led to a resounding success. Cavinkare offers another lesson, too. Its distribution system was and continues to be unique, and in 2014 Cavinkare sought to give its sales and profits a boost by making major investments in its distribution system, embracing literally millions of little shops.

Distribution is of enormous importance in emerging economies. Companies have learned not to allow anyone or anything to come between them and the customer. Consequently they have built distribution systems that tie them closely to the customer. Philips, for instance, in line with its new focus on health and lifestyle, built a distribution system in India that employs thousands of small shopkeepers and distributors who are allocated small territories. The employees are also potential customers and thus provide valuable insights to Philips. The company's distribution system, then, does more than serve the supply chain well; it is also carefully aligned with customer interests, and is a key source of competitive advantage for Philips's new low-cost personal care and kitchen products that are designed and built in India.

Employing Stretch Goals

Another of Jhunjhunwala's lessons, which the GE story also demonstrates, involves the importance of BHAGs (Big Hairy Audacious Goals)[11] to drive and direct breakthroughs in technology and business models. Of course, frugal engineering – which is based on intensive value engineering at the design stage, and rigorously applied lean engineering in the manufacturing process – is needed to meet the price-point challenge. But BHAGs force individuals to break out of the limitations of the linear thinking characteristic of typical frugal engineering. Emerging economies and the needs and purchasing power of the base of the pyramid force firms to explicitly articulate and commit to BHAGs.

BHAGs have been the motivator of many notable breakthrough innovations. The Tata Nano, the least expensive car in the world, is a stunning feat of engineering. Mr Ratan Tata, then chairman of the Tata Group, is reputed to have set the incredibly ambitious goal of offering a $2000 car when he saw a family of four on a motorcycle involved in an accident. Motorcycles commonly carry entire families in countries with low per-capita income.

In the late 1990s and early 2000s, I served as "subject matter expert" for five benchmarking studies of strategic planning, four of which were organized by the APQC (previously known as the American Productivity and Quality Center) and one which was sponsored by the Hong Kong Productivity Council (HKPC). A total of 87 companies sponsored the studies of 22 "best-in-class" companies from across three continents. One of the most striking findings was that the best in class companies stressed the importance of stretch goals in improving performance significantly more than the sponsoring companies who served as a control group.

Achieving stretch goals requires breakthroughs in thinking and practice. Vodafone CZ, operating in the Czech Republic with two larger competitors, set a remarkable goal of "transforming the telecommunications industry."[12] This might seem like hubris, for a relatively small company, operating in a small country, with no in-country R&D capability in telecommunications. But the ambitious goal resulted in Vodafone CZ thinking creatively along the elements of the value chain that it did control. To meet this goal, Vodafone CZ adopted a value proposition that stated simply, "Break all the rules for the customer." Following the adoption of this value proposition, Vodafone CZ introduced practices that transformed the telecommunications business. Customer representatives were empowered to do anything that was required, even break company policies, to remedy problems encountered by customers. There was no limit to the monetary compensation that a representative could offer a customer who had encountered a problem caused by Vodafone CZ. Customers were not required to sign contracts and could, if they wished, shift to another carrier without penalty. Existing customers were given all the incentives offered to new customers.

Vodafone CZ publicly challenged its competitors to adopt its approach to serving the customer. And Vodafone CZ became, for its size, the most profitable telecommunications company in the world.

Reworking the Management System

There is another lesson GE offers us as we develop our approach to fashioning Wicked Strategies. GE has been at the forefront of management expertise since its investment of $4 million (around $45 million in today's dollars) in the early 1950s in a project to identify the key business areas in which companies must perform well in order to be sustainable. This management expertise displays itself in GE's reworking of its management system to support its new strategic emphasis on emerging economies and reverse innovation.[13] According to Immelt and his co-authors (2009), GE revolutionized its management system in order to support the development of breakthrough technologies, which in turn enabled new business models that boosted economic value added. The intent was to develop technology and business model innovations in emerging economies to add value in those markets, and to also bring back these developments to the Triad economies for added competitive advantage and profits. To implement this strategy, GE changed it organization structure to bring new attention to the fast-growing emerging economies, modified its resource allocation and performance measurement practices to focus on disruptive rather than

sustaining innovation, and reaffirmed its commitment to an entrepreneurial, risk-taking management style.

GE had traditionally viewed its financial performance by product
line, focusing on the global revenues and profits of each product line.
In this scheme, each of the emerging economies contributed a small
amount, thus not meriting much management attention or resources.
In order to support its strategy of reverse innovation based on a growing emphasis on emerging markets, GE reoriented its reports to focus
on revenues and profits by country, which increased the significance
of each country and emerging economy in the management's delib-
erations. Country managers gained significance in the organizational
matrix, and consequently they were better able to direct resources,
human and financial, from across the company to support innovation in and for emerging economies. Even the measures of performance changed to support disruptive innovation.

For instance, Immelt expressed reservations about the use of
"market share," which has traditionally been viewed as the most
important and meaningful measure of competitive strength and
strategic performance. The reason for his reservations, beyond the
usual concerns about how to define the market and the changing
nature of the market, were that the market-share measure kept management's attention on the past. The larger the market share, the less
inclined managers would be to accept and employ disruptive innovations. Instead, they would see sustaining innovations as the only
logical way to go, in order to build on their existing strengths. And
as Christensen points out, traditional incremental economic analysis is strongly weighted in favor of sustaining innovation. The fixed
costs and investments needed to create disruptive innovations
will, justifiably, be entered into the decision matrix. In the case of
sustaining innovations, such investments have often been already
incurred and will also justifiably be treated as sunk costs and, as
such, will be irrelevant to the analysis. However, managers conducting the analyses and committing to sustaining innovation will

not be predisposed to recognize and anticipate the potential impact of disruptive technologies, which could very well abruptly end the cash flow projected from existing operations.

GE reworked its performance measurement, planning processes, and organizational structure – in other words its management system – in order to implement its strategy of reverse innovation.

Design Thinking and Data Analytics

There are two relatively novel approaches in management practice and thinking that can assist in developing innovative business models. First is the design thinking[14] process, which seeks to build empathy with the client or customer and stimulate creative responses to the customer's needs. Second is the increasing power of analytics focused on big data.[15] While analysis of big data cannot reveal cause–effect relationships, businesses now are able to derive powerful insights[16] about the customer that can support innovative value propositions. The process of design thinking and the insights derived from big data analytics in combination can facilitate and enhance the creation of innovative business models.

Design thinking starts with an empathetic understanding of the customer's needs. Professor Jhunjhunwala's experience, discussed earlier, reinforces the critical importance of such an understanding. In his case it led him to shift from a competence-based focus on the technology of communication to its use in meeting the health, education, and livelihood needs of India's low-income population. In fact, in all the examples presented in this chapter – Tenet, Arvind, GE, Tata, Vodafone CZ, and Cavinkare – insightfully identifying with and understanding the customer was a common and critically important element in the process of motivating disruptive technologies and building innovative business models.

In addition to empathizing with the customer, design thinking, as described by Jon Kolko,[17] involves developing models that simplify and promote comprehension of the problem, testing and refining possible solutions, accepting uncertainty, and tolerating risk. The experimental, prototyping-based process espoused by design thinking is analogous to the approach to product innovation that employs an experiential process involving improvisation, real-time adaptation, and flexibility. This experimental approach to product innovation was found by Eisenhardt and Tabrizi[18] to be more effective than rational, compression models in accelerating adaptive processes in organizations

Embracing design thinking requires both creativity and courage. In later chapters we will describe simple but powerful techniques such as possibility scenarios, which support and facilitate adoption of core elements of the design thinking process.

COMPILING THE RESPONSES: INNOVATIVE BUSINESS MODELS

Perhaps the most important lesson that can be derived from looking at the examples we discussed, which I have deliberately not made explicit until now so that you would – I hope – arrive at the same conclusion on your own, is that what appears to be a dire threat to organizations can, with a ton of courage and a modicum of creativity, be alchemized into a powerful and generous source of competitive advantage and added economic value.

The practices for dealing with disruptive technologies that have been discussed in this chapter suggest guidelines that enable organizations to transmute disruption and chaos into cash flow, and to seek and embrace disruptive technologies as the foundation for *innovative business models*. These guidelines are:

1 Specify extraordinarily ambitious goals.
2 Support an entrepreneurial, risk-taking culture in the firm.

3 Relate empathetically to the customer.
4 Integrate social responsibility into the business model.
5 Utilize design thinking and data analytics.
6 Explore disruptive possibilities along the entire value chain.
7 Add dynamically to the array of capabilities that the firm possesses.
8 Implement supportive organizational structures, and planning and control systems.

These responses together combine to create *innovative business models* that incorporate *disruptive technologies*.

We will elaborate further on the necessary characteristics and process of developing Wicked Strategies in later chapters, after first exploring the implications of *conflicted stakeholders* (chapter 3) formed by the intersections of innovation and shared value, and *unknowable futures* (chapter 4) formed by the intersection of shared value and globalization.

CHAPTER 3

Conflicted Stakeholders: Partnerships and Possibilities

Difficulties are meant to rouse, not discourage. The human spirit is to grow strong by conflict.

William Ellery Channing

In organizations, the interaction of the imperative of *innovation* and the commitment to *shared value* generates *conflicted stakeholders*. This is because innovation can enable and even require changes in the business model. New business models will generate value in novel ways, changing the relevance and importance of existing stakeholders, requiring a fresh and different understanding of how the value will be shared. Conflict between stakeholders can reasonably be expected to happen as a result. Earlier, in our discussion of disruptive technologies, which result from the interaction of innovation and globalization, the point was made that though disruptive technologies may at first glance appear to threaten the firm's viability, they can, if embraced as the basis for innovative business models, prove to be a powerful source of competitive advantage and economic value. Conflicted stakeholders, if motivated and enabled to co-create value, can similarly serve as a source of competitive advantage and economic value.

FROM CONFLICTED STAKEHOLDERS TO THE CO-CREATION OF VALUE

Co-creation is an inherently attractive, beneficent, and non-threatening prospect that may help generate the innovative business models that embrace disruptive technologies. Co-creation of value is something the firm can choose to do or not to do. Disruptive technologies, in contrast, may often resemble an unavoidable force of nature. They can happen without warning, without the firm's involvement, and can threaten the firm's viability. To paraphrase a popular but scatological bumper sticker, "Disruption Happens!" And this is why managing and creating innovative business models, though daunting and difficult, is critically important. It is better for the firm itself to make its existing business model obsolete by fashioning a superior, disruptive business model than to let circumstances or competitors do it. Owning and managing the disruption creates replacement sources of value that enable the firm to survive and possibly thrive.

Even so, co-creation of value is often readily viewed by managers as a desirable option. Gary Hamel, in his book *Leading the Revolution*,[1] lists the many benefits of co-creation. The benefits, according to Hamel, include increased innovation capacity and velocity, reduced risk, more and better ideas for development, and reduced time for commercializing ideas.

To understand and support co-creation of value we will consider:

1   The role of stakeholders in co-creation of value
2   How value is received or earned by stakeholders engaged in co-creation
3   How to manage stakeholders involved in the co-creation process
4   Building alliances to co-create value

5 Prompting co-creation of value within the firm
6 Promoting an innovation ecosystem to accelerate co-creation
   of value

The Role of Stakeholders in Co-Creation

Innovation is an imperative, and we have seen that in order to
manage disruption it is necessary to become one with the customer.
This means that collaborating and co-creating value with customers
is desirable if not essential.[2] Much of the co-creation activity that is
described in the press, books, and articles relates to innovations in
marketing, through branding, product and service variations, and
packaging. But if the firm is committed to *shared value*, co-creation
of value with other stakeholders, in addition to customers, is a
must. A good example is the "value constellation" proposed by
Normann and Ramirez,[3] which engages a range of stakeholders in
"co-producing" value at various stages in the firm's value chain.

Most pertinent to our discussion is the notion of "innovating for
shared value."[4] Effective engagement of selected stakeholders can
enhance the stakeholders' sense of ownership and identification
with the firm, as well as, of course, unearthing opportunities for the
addition of economic value.

Co-creation of value with selected stakeholders can be viewed as
the equivalent of social entrepreneurship for the for-profit sector.
It could create partnerships that give the firm access to resources
and influence that would not otherwise be available. GE worked
with government and customers to develop a cost-effective, envi-
ronmentally friendly approach to water usage for oil extraction in
Canada, which set the stage for future partnerships with and access
to government resources. When Arvind worked with destitute
farmers to help them earn a living by teaching them how to grow
organic cotton in unirrigated lands that were at the mercy of the
vagaries of the monsoon season, they worked with and nurtured

valuable, significant, long-term partners such as the Tata Group and the state government.

Earning and Receiving Value from Co-Creation

Building long-term partnerships and value is important for tapping the potential synergy between innovation and shared value. Consequently, the co-creation processes we need to design and employ are quite different from open-sourcing and crowd-sourcing processes. Open sourcing and crowd sourcing tend to be technology based and do work well in certain situations. Open sourcing works well when what is being sought is a plethora of ideas for something like a brand name, or small contributions from individuals. It works well for software development when the four freedoms[5] of the Free Software Foundation (FSF) are adopted. The motivations of participants[6] in open sourcing approaches are usually personal, are competitive with regard to other participants, and are not necessarily conducive to a long-term involvement. These motivations are not meaningful for the types of effective, stakeholder-serving innovation that is the purpose of the co-creation in which we are interested.

The co-creation we seek to employ is a defined, distinct, and collaborative effort to promote value-creating innovation by a selected set of individuals who possess relevant knowledge or perspectives. Possibilities for such co-creation abound. In the context of developing Wicked Strategies, co-creation can focus on:

- Elements of the business model, ranging from the value proposition to the measures of performance
- The activities in the generic value chain – both supporting elements, such as technology, and primary activities, such as marketing and distribution
- Connections with other firms – e.g., suppliers, customers, and alliance partners

- Interactions between departments and functions within the firm
- Stakeholders who are significant in terms of their potential impact on the firm, or who are affected by the activities of the firm.

An example of co-creating an organization's value proposition was an exercise conducted by a client. The firm's business, which engaged and brought thousands of engineers and managers to the United States, had been deeply affected by the 9/11 attack on the World Trade Center in New York City and the resulting restrictions on travel and entry into the United States. The firm had numerous planning meetings to figure out how to reposition its business to respond to the new realities, but the personnel in the firm were having a hard time coming up with reasonable and promising alternatives. The firm's CEO came to the conclusion that fresh thinking was required. His solution was to have a detailed case study of the firm prepared, detailing its history, strategy, resources, and the changing context that it faced. The CEO, employing his own and the consultant's contacts, identified fifteen executives from other companies who had a reputation for creative thinking. The C-suite executives from the firm, as well as several managers from various departments and functions, joined the fifteen invited executives to discuss the case study, with a view to identifying mission and strategic alternatives as well as possible significant operational enhancements. A host of credible ideas emerged during the discussion, stimulated by the invited executives. These ideas were later vetted by the CEO and the consultant, and reviewed by a large number of managers in the firm. The firm adopted a promising new value proposition and also decided to implement several of the operational enhancements that had come up during the discussion.

Managing Stakeholders

Inviting executives from other firms to participate in a co-creation process is an unusual practice, though it worked very well for this firm. Stakeholders such as suppliers, distributors and customers are usually involved in co-creation exercises. When identifying stakeholders to participate in such exercises it is useful to employ a classification scheme such as the matrix presented in figure 3.1.

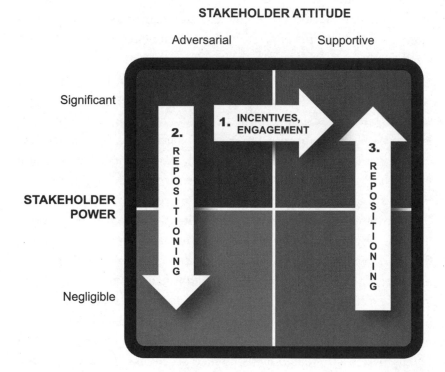

Figure 3.1 Stakeholder Classification Matrix

The primary focus has to be on stakeholders who are powerful. An objective of the co-creation processes should be to seek outcomes that would:

• Move the powerful, adversarial stakeholders to a different relationship by providing incentives (arrow "1" in figure 3.1);

- Offer opportunities for the powerful, adversarial stakeholders to be better engaged with the firm (arrow "1" in figure 3.1);
- Strategically reposition the firm (arrow "2" in figure 3.1) to reduce the power of adversarial stakeholders;
- Strategically reposition the firm (arrow "3" in figure 3.1) to make supportive stakeholders more significant; or,
- In the case of powerful supportive stakeholders, offer opportunities for even better engagement, and reposition the firm to enhance their power.

All of these moves need to be borne in mind when making any strategic decision. The relevance and value of the perspectives highlighted by this matrix are clearly evident in the context of making a choice regarding which country to enter, or deciding in which community to locate a plant. Keeping this matrix in mind would also help improve strategic decisions where the identity and potential role of stakeholders is not readily obvious.

Co-creation by connecting elements of the firm's value chain with those of suppliers or customers can be very productive. Alcoa is an excellent example of such co-creation of value. Alcoa partnering with Audi to create the radical, space-age, aluminum automobile frame was a breakthrough that could only have been achieved by co-creation. Similarly, Alcoa, working with Pittsburgh Brewing, created a unique, deep-drawn aluminum bottle, the novelty value of which greatly boosted the sales of the IC Light brand of beer. And in a recent and highly visible partnership, Alcoa worked with Ford to replace steel with aluminum in the body of Ford's most important and profitable product, its F-150 pickup truck.

There are several possible connections across the value chain that can support co-creation. The design of components or products can be coordinated with the manufacturing or marketing functions of the customer. Logistics and distribution can hook up with the purchasing function of the customer.

Building Alliances

Alliances provide a highly effective framework for co-creation. They are particularly helpful when entering into or creating new markets. In particular, alliances are a way of acquiring or accessing competencies that are needed to handle the disruptions likely to occur in emerging economies.

In building alliances for co-creation, Rosabeth Moss Kanter[7] offers some important guidelines. She urges firms to partner only with the finest firms. Effective alliances can only be built on a foundation of trust. Having the finest partner with which to work motivates and creates such a climate.

Kanter identifies levels of interaction between partnering firms that suggest opportunities for and facilitators of co-creation. The levels suggested are (1) strategic, (2) tactical, (3) operational, (4) interpersonal, and (5) cultural.

The *strategic level* suggests co-creating new markets. An example is the catalogue flower business that was created by Ruth Owades. Her startup company, Calyx and Corolla, became a great success because of the alliances she carefully instituted and nurtured. Her experience in the catalogue business gave her the credibility to pull together FedEx and pioneering flower growers to create an entirely new business model for selling flowers. This strategic level of co-creation develops and affirms a common understanding of the new target market, which is shared by firms in the alliance.

The *tactical level* refers to the projects that the partners work on together to exploit their target market. The different competencies as well as the complementary competencies possessed by the partners sustain the projects. Differences could be a source of friction, but, in beneficial partnerships, they make the alliance more productive and improve the outcomes of co-creation.

The *operational level* focuses on the processes that need to be in place to support co-creation. Communications technology could play an important role here.

The *interpersonal level* addresses the relationships between individuals across the companies in the alliance. Often a close relationship between champions of the project (*tactical level*) in each of the companies involved is what initially sustains the alliance and supports co-creation.

Finally, the *cultural level* recognizes that differences in perspective and knowledge are what make co-creation happen; there has to be mutual respect for and acceptance of the partner's differences, not responses that cause alienation.

Co-Creation within the Firm

Co-creation potential that exists within the firm should also be tapped. Many companies accomplish this through project teams with diverse membership. The famous Team Taurus, which created one of Ford Motor Company's most successful models, included engineers with a variety of expertise, designers, marketers, and accountants. It is quite common for firms to follow this "super team" approach to commercialize new technologies. Lockheed Martin, for example, has its "Skunk Works" – an alias inspired by a moonshine factory of the same name in the comic strip Li'l Abner – which are "super teams" located physically separate from the main operations of the firm, sometimes on a secret or confidential basis, to create major new and superior products. The Lockheed Skunk Works produced breakthrough aircraft such as the U-2 and the SR-71 Blackbird, which are considered to be some of the most advanced aircraft ever made.

It is interesting to note that breakthroughs seem to require a great deal of autonomy and a separation from the main line of business.

IBM, for instance, found that it had to develop the PC using a small team, kept away from its headquarters in Armonk, NY. IBM was very much a mainframe manufacturer in those days, and the PC would have found little support at headquarters.

Skunk works and super teams function as collateral organizations, separate from the main organization. In effect, they are delinked from the inertia, or the momentum, of the primary organization. Their existence can also be time-bound, tied to a strategic transformational project, with deadlines for implementation. These components of the organization can be added or dropped when the strategic transformational initiatives are initiated, terminated, or absorbed by the primary organization. They represent a modular approach to organizational design and structure.

This modular approach to structure can be extremely supportive of the transformation demanded by disruptive innovations discussed in the previous chapter. Skunk works and super teams insulate entrepreneurial ventures and transformational innovations from the primary organization's emotional investment in and commitment to existing technologies and business models.

The Innovation Ecosystem for Co-Creating Value

Skunk works and super teams are important as internal means of structuring and stimulating the co-creation of innovative value. On the external front, a powerful engine of innovation, which involves a constellation of firms and other organizations, has evolved over the years. The highly interactive diversity of capabilities that drives innovation in skunk works also works for groups of companies. This engine of innovation has its roots in a framework that Michael Porter highlighted when he analyzed the competitive advantage of nations.[8] He identified the importance of related and supplier industries, which are the foundation for the formation of industry clusters such as Hollywood and Bollywood for movies, Detroit and Stuttgart for automobiles, and Silicon Valley and Bangalore for information technology. Clusters are a static concept that evolved into the notion of innovation ecosystems. Innovation ecosystems are a dynamic mix of small companies, large companies, startups, diverse services, venture capital, research institutions, universities, and supportive government policy. Innovation ecosystems are a hotbed of innovation and co-created value.

Innovation surges when connections are made between ecosystems in different industries. Dramatic examples visible on a daily basis are the innovations resulting from connecting the automobile and information technology industries. Similarly, connections between IT and healthcare have boosted innovation at all stages of the health-industry value chain from research to client records.

There is a related phenomenon: connections between ecosystems in the same industry, but operating in different markets, stimulate innovation. That phenomenon is what companies like GE and Philips are relying on to support their goals of reverse innovation. This phenomenon reinforces the idea discussed earlier that operations in emerging economies and low-end markets can foster disruptive innovation, which, if managed well, can strengthen the competitive advantage of firms.

Global communities of knowledge can be set up to foster innovation. Royal Dutch Shell, which was a best-in-class example of strategic planning (especially scenario building) that I had the opportunity to study in detail, has for many years used virtual communities of knowledge to share information about best practices in planning across countries. Another example with which I have personal familiarity is the Low Voltage DC (LVDC) Forum of the Institute of Electrical and Electronics Engineers (IEEE), which brings together companies, universities, research institutions, consultants, and government bodies. The members of the LVDC forum seek to establish standards, engage with government regulators, and jointly implement pilot projects. They share the knowledge emerging from the research conducted by individual members, which could support their common objectives and programs. These communities of knowledge are powerful catalysts and accelerators of innovation, and the commercialization of innovation.

COMPILING THE RESPONSES: CO-CREATING VALUE

Co-creation processes to support innovation for multiple stakeholders can play a major role in developing Wicked Strategies. The variety of ways in which co-creation can take place, the diversity of stakeholders and entities that could be involved, and the assortment of benefits that can be derived require that the process be carefully designed and managed. A diverse set of capabilities that interact in positive ways are at the root of value-generating innovation. Co-creation can be applied to develop fundamental value propositions, visions, strategies, competencies, products and services, business models, and measures of performance.

Based on what we have discussed in this chapter, certain conditions are required in order for co-creation to occur. They are as follows:

1 The parties involved need to be different, though complementary and mutually respectful. Co-creation thrives on differences, and from this vantage point, conflicted stakeholders offer value-adding potential.
2 Stakeholders need to be carefully managed, which is to say, consciously identified, analyzed, and co-incentivized. The priorities of powerful, adversarial stakeholders need to be recognized and addressed.
3 Stakeholders, including suppliers, business partners, and customers, can be engaged in co-creating value and supporting innovation at selected stages across the entire value chain.

4 Alliances need to be built with firms that have complementary capabilities.
5 The structural context in which co-creation takes place within an organization is important. Autonomy is necessary and skunk works or super teams are effective. Also effective is a modular organization structure that is designed to add or drop semi-autonomous units to manage risk, to bypass organizational blinders and inertia, and to enable organizational transformation.
6 Innovation ecosystems that include a variety of organizations need to be nurtured; linked innovation ecosystems that span industries and different markets are especially creative and desirable.

Co-creation, because it involves and engages diverse stakeholders and offers the possibility of benefiting from disruptive innovation, is a strong and meaningful response to the challenge of wicked problems. The third and final challenge – *unknowable futures* – is discussed next in chapter 4.

CHAPTER 4

Unknowable Futures: Risks and Responses

The trouble with our times is that the future is not what it used to be.

Paul Valéry

The interaction of *globalization* and *shared value* creates a potent brew that has a formidable impact on organizations. Companies embarking on globalization are thrust literally and metaphorically into a world of uncertainty and complexity. When the power and priorities of multiple and diverse stakeholders interact with the complexities and uncertainties of globalization, the result is a recipe for decision paralysis. Not only does the firm's future become difficult to predict, but the extreme uncertainty and complexity that accompany globalization, when compounded by the different perspectives and priorities of diverse stakeholders, may lead to a chaotic ambiguity where the future is not only unpredictable but essentially unknowable. Some argue, for example, that even God may find it difficult to predict what will happen next year in the Middle East!

This third interaction between the mega-forces, *unknown futures*, is very different than the other two interactions, *conflicted stakeholders* and *disruptive technologies*. Differences between *conflicted stakeholders* can spark creativity. Well-managed co-creation offers the promise of encouraging interaction between important, though conflicted, stakeholders. Such interaction can be the path to identifying, acquiring, or developing needed competencies to develop new products and enter new markets, which generates economic value that benefits and reconciles conflicted stakeholders. *Disruptive technologies* present more of a challenge, but still offer the potential for adding value. Traditional management processes and decision analyses are inclined to favor sustaining innovation over disruptive innovation, opening the firm to the possibility of staying with a business model that could become obsolete because of disruptive technologies and business models embraced and introduced by competitors. But, if welcomed and thoughtfully managed, disruptive technologies can boost competitive advantage and economic sustainability.

Unknowable futures offer no such promises of a possible upside. Instead, they offer an unvarnished, unequivocal challenge. This challenge needs to be overcome; much like ensuring the presence of hygiene factors in American psychologist F.I. Herzberg's[1] two-factor theory of motivation. If the challenge that *unknowable futures* pose is not met, the economic value generated by the firm will be constrained or reduced, and the firm's viability may be threatened.

Unknowable futures are the reason why firms that employ the best of the traditional planning processes and analytical techniques are sometimes unable to gain any traction. To paraphrase German Field Marshal Helmuth von Moltke's famous dictum: "No strategic plan survives contact with an *unknowable future!*"

Traditional tools of strategic analysis are designed to understand and predict competitive industry environments (e.g., five-forces analysis) or develop differentiation maneuvers for an anticipated future (e.g., generic value chains linked with customers' or supplier's chains). However, they are patently unsuited for and utterly helpless to deal with an unknowable future.

Additional approaches also fall short. Conducting strategic planning exercises more frequently, requiring additional analysis, separating strategic thinking from action planning, or using carefully developed ROI projections as a basis for selecting strategies are of little worth when challenged by this degree of uncertainty and complexity. Unknowable futures are no less unambiguous when subjected to more frequent traditional analyses. A greater degree of analysis is a waste of time and effort if it is predicated on incorrect or questionable assumptions. Understanding the implications and the implementation challenges of new strategies is next to impossible without simultaneously exploring the feasibility of actions required to fulfil the strategy. Faced with the probability of incorrect assumptions, unanticipated developments, and undeveloped action plans, employing ROI projections as the criterion for selecting an optimum strategy is dysfunctional at worst and an exercise in futility at best.

Therefore, when we review the thrust of efforts frequently used by companies to make their strategic planning more effective, the fruitlessness of their efforts in the context of unknowable futures should be apparent for the following reasons:

- Changing the scheduled frequency of strategic planning exercises does not make an unknowable future less so.
- Specifying greater detail in processes inherently designed to function in the context of a likely future is unhelpful when the future cannot be predicted.
- Evaluating strategies based on their bottom-line impact is likely to be misleading when the understanding of the profit model – cause–effect relationships – is based on an assumption of a future that is essentially a mirage.

FROM AN UNKNOWABLE FUTURE TO FEED-FORWARD

What then can one do in the face of an unknowable future? A couple of decades ago, in my consulting, I became aware of the ineffectiveness of then available techniques that were intended to delineate or deal with an anticipated future. I started searching for, researching, designing, and documenting planning processes that could better manage an unknowable future.[2] These writings led to my being contacted by Dr William (Bill) Gilmore, an astrophysicist by training, who, because of his work experience with large, complex software projects, had encountered similar problems. We co-authored an article[3] that deconstructed what we categorized as "wicked" problems, and we recommended processes and techniques that would, we believed, be responsive to these issues. These processes and techniques are better informed now by the multi-year, multi-country research projects and extensive consulting I have done with more than 100 organizations, ranging from Fortune 500 companies to theological seminaries. The processes and approaches that are proven to address wicked problems are identified in the following sections.

Identity Definition

Unknowable futures make it impossible to project the trajectories of industry, domain, technology, product, and market evolution. These traditional core elements of strategy no longer serve as reliable and enduring descriptors of the future organization and its strategy. What is needed instead are guidelines, touchstones, or lenses for strategic decision making that can transcend disruptions and also provide guidance in never-before-experienced contexts. It is necessary to rethink and redefine what is *core* to, *enduring*, and *distinctive* about the firm. In later chapters, we will develop the construct of "identity," which possesses these three characteristics, and which consequently transcends disruptive changes. The components of identity include the *values*, which are *core* to the firm; its *aspirations* (or vision), which are *enduring*; and its *competencies*, which make it *distinctive*. I will also offer an approach to converting this construct of "identity" into a decision matrix that can support the process of formulating Wicked Strategies and corresponding guidance on resource allocation.

Visioning

There is truth in clichés, and the classic aphorism that has become a cliché in the global business environment – "When you can't predict the future, create it" – certainly applies here. When operating in the environment of *unknowable futures*, creating a desired future is the goal, and the organization's vision is its expression of a desired future. The potential for visioning a desired future derives from an organization's identity, its raison d'être. The organization's *core values* (e.g., sharing economic value added equitably among stakeholders; demonstrating simplicity in purpose and operations; caring for the environment) provide meaning and guidance to the vision. The organization's *enduring aspirations* (e.g., leadership in technology; innovativeness in value propositions; dominance in market share; growth significantly higher than selected market indices; empathetically serving customer needs; enhancing the quality of life at the bottom of the pyramid; synergistically integrating economic value and social benefit) are what give substance to the vision. Finally, the organization's *distinctive competencies* determine the viability of the vision and enable its realization.

The classic planning processes and variations, such as MIT professor J.B. Quinn's logical incrementalism,[4] as well as feed-forward processes (to be discussed in chapter 7), employ visions and visioning as part of the process.

Actions to Strategy Sequence

The organization's commitment to *shared value* exacerbates and compounds the complexity and uncertainty arising from the forces of *globalization*. Stakeholder management, as detailed in chapter 3's discussion about *conflicted stakeholders* and the related Stakeholder Classification Matrix (see figure 3.1), is a useful starting point for responding to this challenge. For instance, as the matrix suggests, moving powerful stakeholders who are adversarial to a more supportive stance can be attempted by providing incentives or by meaningfully engaging them in the decision-making processes of the firm.

When faced with an *unknowable future*, another response relevant to the challenge posed by multiple stakeholders who do not share the same goals or values was suggested by Charles Lindblom.[5] Lindblom identified the intriguing reality that while stakeholders may have different priorities or values, there are certain actions that all may agree are acceptable. For instance, governments, NGOs, and firms, though their values, priorities, and motivations may be different, may all agree that providing financial services to people at the bottom of the pyramid is a good thing. A set of actions on which diverse stakeholders agree can serve as the basis for a Wicked Strategy. Lindblom calls this action to strategy sequence a branch-to-root approach; it is the reverse of the classic approach, which is to proceed from strategy to actions, which Lindblom characterizes as root-to-branch.

While Lindblom did justifiably claim that this approach is rooted in science, his labeling of the process as "muddling through," while arguably appropriate and evocative, did not contribute to the popularization of this powerful and insightful approach. Also contributing to the lack of widespread awareness and acceptance of this approach was the fact that Lindblom labored in the policy-sciences vineyard, rather than in the business arena. However, an article that applied this actions to strategy approach to the business arena was authored by Robert H. Hayes.[6] He described this approach as "Strategic Planning – Forward in Reverse"; again a less than felicitous label.

Robust Actions

There is also the concept of *robust actions*, which work effectively in multiple contexts. The hallmark of unknowable futures is that while no specific future may be identified in the context of the complexity and uncertainty caused by the incendiary mix of globalization and shared value, it may be possible to speculate on a variety of different scenarios that conceivably could emerge. Experience has shown that there is a common set of actions, *robust actions*,[7] which make sense and contribute to added value in each and every one of the possible scenarios that are conjectured. Robust actions offer an escape hatch for organizations trapped in decision paralysis. A planning process for identifying robust actions will be presented in chapter 7, which focuses on *feed-forward* processes and systems.

Real Options

Real options essentially require an organization to make the minimum investment necessary to enter and retain a foothold in a business opportunity or a strategic initiative, while gathering information that sheds more light on the context and the future. When greater clarity is achieved, a more confident determination can be made of whether and how to go ahead with the business opportunity or strategic initiative. Major investments and more defined commitments can then be made. A real-options approach or mindset can provide the flexibility that firms need to respond more effectively to the complexity and uncertainty that characterize an *unknowable future*.

Robust actions serve as a foundation for a real-options approach. A real-options[8] approach recognizes that the veils of uncertainty and the knots of complexity may lift and unravel over time to the point where a reasonable projection of a likely future may be made and resources may be committed in anticipation of this future happening. Robust actions enable organizations to move forward, while waiting for information that clarifies the future to the point where risks can be calculated and reasoned investment decisions can be made. The alternative is to be paralysed with indecision, or pressured into making investments with wholly inadequate information.

Real-Time Issue Management

Guided by its identity, motivated by its vision, and empowered by robust actions, an organization that steps into an unknowable future may be as well positioned as possible, but unanticipated problems, and sudden opportunities, will present themselves. Engaging in annual planning processes, as most organizations do, cannot cope with the reality and inevitability of randomly emerging strategic issues. In place of episodic planning processes, a continuous issue management[9] process is demanded by the nature of an unpredictable future. Real-time issue management, as opposed to episodic strategic planning at preset intervals, is logically consistent with and supportive of "scientific muddling through" and the real-options approach.

Rapid Prototyping/Experimentation

Concomitant with real-time issue management is the need to test the organization's chosen responses to the emerging issues. It is important to learn as quickly as possible whether the responses are effective. A rapid prototyping approach to the new strategic initiatives and business models is of relevance here. The mindset is one of experimentation, of hypothesis testing, where the object is to learn and improve, as opposed to declaring failure or defeat. The effectiveness of this experiential approach to accelerating effective innovation has been supported by Eisenhardt and Tabrizi's[10] research.

Design thinking[11] can undergird hypothesis development and experimentation. Empathy with the customer, which initiates the design-thinking process, can lead to creative and rich hypotheses, supporting innovative business models. As mentioned earlier, data analytics too can be a powerful tool for developing insightful hypotheses.

In a feed-forward context, carefully planned initiatives are meaningfully viewed as *experiments*. Whether the initiative works well or not, it can provide valuable insights into cause–effect relationships and the validity of underlying assumptions.

COMPILING THE RESPONSES: FEED-FORWARD PROCESSES

The approaches and techniques to respond to unknowable futures are as follows:

1 Identity definition – articulating what is core, enduring, and distinctive about the firm, which can transcend discontinuities and disruptions
2 Visioning – defining a future that would motivate and guide decision making
3 Actions to strategy sequence – the branch-to-root process or "scientific muddling through"
4 Robust actions – effective in multiple scenarios and contexts
5 Real options – building flexibility into strategic decisions; postponing major commitments until better information is obtained
6 Real-time issue management – continuous strategic planning triggered by issues as they emerge or appear on the horizon.
7 Rapid prototyping/experimentation – testing the organization's responses to emerging issues, problems, and opportunities

As was evident in the discussions, these approaches and techniques work in close concert with one another. These responses to an *unknowable future* align with a feed-forward[12] approach to planning and control. Feed-forward-based planning and control processes work from the future backward, as opposed to the classical, feedback approach, which seeks to draw lessons from the past. Feed-forward is an important and powerful approach to meeting the challenge of wicked problems and will be described in detail in chapter 7.

PART 2

THE ORGANIZATIONAL ARCHITECTURE FOR WICKED STRATEGIES

The Foundation of Wicked Strategic Management: Melding Innovative Business Models, Co-Creation of Value, and Feed-Forward Processes

Life was simple before World War II. After that, we had systems.

Grace Hopper

In the previous three chapters we identified responses to three strategic challenges that give rise to wicked problems. The responses to each of the challenges were developed separately. In this chapter we will aggregate and review the responses developed to these strategic challenges, identify and eliminate redundancies, and then cluster related responses together.

We will integrate the opportunities created by *disruptive technologies*, the possibilities offered by *conflicted stakeholders*, and the responses to *unknowable futures* discussed in the previous three chapters. *Innovative business models* represent the opportunity arising from disruptive technologies; *co-creation of value* represents the possibility that motivates conflicted stakeholders; and *feed-forward processes* are the response to unknowable futures.

Innovative business models, co-creation of value, and feed-forward processes need to work in synch in order to maximize their effect when incorporated into Wicked Strategies. We will examine the elements of these three to detect common patterns, identify interactions, and link related actions and techniques in order to create an integrative framework that can effectively and efficiently support the development and deployment of Wicked Strategies.

To initiate the identification of commonalities, we will juxtapose and cluster the actions, approaches, and techniques developed in the previous three chapters. For ease of reference, these actions, approaches, and techniques are reproduced below.

For innovative business models we identified the elements as:

1   Specify incredibly ambitious goals.
2   Support an entrepreneurial, risk-taking culture in the firm.
3   Relate empathetically to the customer in order to create disruptive business models.
4   Integrate social responsibility into the business model.
5   Utilize design thinking and data analytics.
6   Explore disruptive possibilities along the entire value chain.
7   Add dynamically to the array of capabilities possessed by the firm.
8   Implement supportive organizational structures, and planning and control systems.

For co-creation of value we identified the elements as:

1   The parties involved need to be different, though complementary and mutually respectful. Co-creation thrives on differences, and from this vantage point, conflicted stakeholders offer value-adding potential.
2   Stakeholders need to be co-incentivized; the priorities of powerful, adversarial stakeholders need to be recognized and addressed.
3   Stakeholders, including suppliers, business partners, and customers, need to be engaged in co-creating value and supporting innovation at selected stages across the entire value chain.
4   Alliances need to be built with firms that have complementary capabilities.

5 The structural context in which co-creation takes place within an organization is important. Autonomy is necessary and skunk works are effective; so a modular organization structure that is designed to add or drop semi-autonomous units to manage risk, bypass organizational blinders and inertia, and enable organizational transformation is needed to support co-creation, as well as to adopt disruptive innovations.

6 Innovation ecosystems that include a variety of organizations need to be nurtured, linked innovation ecosystems that span industries and different markets are especially creative and desirable.

For feed-forward processes we identified the elements as:

1 Identity definition – articulating what is core, enduring, and distinctive about the firm, which can transcend discontinuities and disruptions

2 Visioning – defining a future that would motivate and guide decision making

3 Actions to strategy sequence – the branch-to-root process or "scientific muddling through"

4 Robust actions – that are effective in multiple scenarios and contexts

5 Real options – building flexibility into strategic decisions; postponing major commitments until better information is obtained

6 Real-time issue management – continuous strategic planning triggered by issues as they emerge or appear on the horizon.

7 Rapid prototyping/experimentation – testing the organization's responses to emerging issues, problems, and opportunities

In table 5.1, each "Construct" row contains similar elements drawn from innovative business models, co-creation of value, and feed-forward processes.

Table 5.1 The Foundation of Wicked Strategic Management

	Focus of Wicked Strategies		
Elements of the architecture	Innovative business models (Disruptive technologies)	Co-creation of value (Conflicted stakeholders)	Feed-forward systems (Unknowable futures)
Construct 1 **Identity**	Set stretch goals – BHAGs Support an entrepreneurial risk-taking culture Build a dynamic array of capabilities	Recognize, engage, and embrace diverse stakeholders	Articulate identity – core values, enduring aspirations, and distinctive competencies Support an entrepreneurial, risk-taking culture
Construct 2 **Feed-forward**	Embrace disruptive technologies and innovation along entire value chain Incorporate social responsibility into the business model Relate empathetically to the customer – focusing on unserved needs Utilize design thinking Redesign planning and control, and human resource systems	Manage stakeholders – engage, incentivize, and reposition Promote and manage alliances Build partnerships at selected stages across the entire value chain Nurture innovation ecosystems	Engage in visioning Focus on unique and unserved customer needs – becoming one with the customer Identify robust actions Adopt a real-options mindset Employ real-time issue management
Construct 3 **Modular structure**	Redesign organizational structure Build a dynamic array of capabilities Experiment in the field	Connect innovation ecosystems Employ skunk works and superteams	Employ skunk works, collateral organizations, and project teams for experimentation and rapid prototyping

By juxtaposing related actions, approaches and techniques that support innovative business models, co-creating value, and feed-forward processes, three constructs readily emerge. The three constructs that are manifested are described below:

The *first construct* includes the following:

- Articulate identity – core values, enduring aspirations, and distinctive competencies
- Recognize and embrace diverse stakeholders

- Set stretch goals – BHAGs
- Support an entrepreneurial, risk-taking culture
- Build a dynamic array of capabilities

This cluster of responses is oriented to meeting the need to have a stable and inspirational basis for making decisions; a way for the organization to define its raison d'être in the context of rapid and unpredictable shifts in environmental contexts and wicked strategic issues. It incorporates values, aspirations, and competencies – three elements that have often been combined into a construct called *identity*. This construct embodies the core (values), enduring (aspirations), and distinctive (competencies) elements that characterize and distinguish an organization.

The *second construct* includes the following imperatives for companies to follow:

- Engage in visioning
- Redesign planning and control, and human resource systems
- Employ real-time issue management
- Embrace disruptive technologies and innovation along the entire value chain
- Incorporate social responsibility into the business model
- Relate empathetically to the customer
- Focus on unique and unserved customer needs; becoming one with the customer
- Manage stakeholders – engage, incentivize, and reposition
- Promote and manage alliances
- Nurture innovation ecosystems
- Identify robust actions
- Adopt a real-options mindset

This second construct incorporates the responses that offer a way to plan and control programs and activities when past experience provides little, no, or misleading guidance, and when the future is unpredictable, and even unknowable. It naturally maps well onto the elements of *feed-forward* processes discussed in chapter 4.

The *third construct* includes the following imperatives for companies to follow:

- Redesign organizational structure
- Employ skunk works, collateral organizations, super teams, and project teams for experimentation and rapid prototyping
- Experiment in the field
- Connect innovation ecosystems
- Build a dynamic array of capabilities

While existing businesses will continue to be effectively supported, the third construct involves modifications and additions to the firm's organizational structure, competencies, and related activities, all of which are intended to support change and transformation. The modifications and additions essentially create a *modular structure* that enables and motivates organizational transformation.

These three constructs – identity, feed-forward and modular structure – together create and symbiotically support Wicked Strategies. These three constructs embody the set of instruments that managers can employ to create the Wicked Strategies that meet the challenges of the mega-forces and add value for the firm. They are the components that constitute the organizational architecture for strategic management in the face of wicked problems.

The logical derivation of these three constructs, starting with the strategic challenges that create wicked problems, offers the promise of dealing with wicked problems at their source. The constructs support innovation in business models, co-creation of value, and feed-forward processes, transmuting the strategic challenges into potential competitive advantage.

This combination of constructs forms a framework, which we will label "feed-forward." The proposed feed-forward framework is designed to develop Wicked Strategies that are calculated to respond to, pre-empt, or transmute wicked problems. The feed-forward framework is diagrammed in figure 5.1.

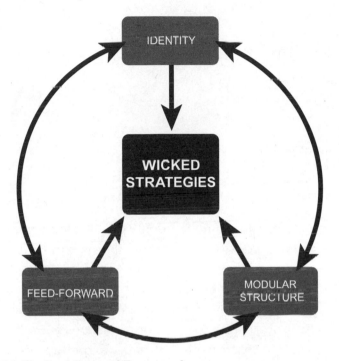

Figure 5.1 The Feed-Forward Framework

Chapters 6, 7, and 8 will discuss identity, feed-forward, and modular structure in the detail that is necessary to employ them effectively in developing and deploying Wicked Strategies. Chapter 9 will focus on linking the three constructs to create the feed-forward framework. Chapter 10 will demonstrate the application of the feed-forward framework.

CHAPTER 6

Identity: Illuminating Decision Making

When I discover who I am, I'll be free.

Ralph Ellison

The need for firms to define an identity is beyond compelling – it is an absolute necessity.[1] In a world that is constantly changing because of myriad forces, including globalization, innovation, and shared value, conventional ways of defining an organization are obsolete or have ephemeral meaning. If strategy is understood to be the construct that harmonizes organizations with their environments, and the construct that illuminates and guides decision making, then having an enduring and evocative understanding of the organization and its raison d'être is necessary. Identity, the first construct developed to respond to the challenges resulting from the three mega-forces, meets this need.

The task of defining a firm's identity, at first glance, appears to be complex and formidable, because we need to find a simple and powerful way of defining the firm that accomplishes the following:

• Insightfully describes the organization, employing dimensions that have strategic import – it has to capture what is *distinctive* about the organization.

- Has substance and meaning that transcends repositioning and transformation of the organization – it has to be *enduring* in the face of disruptive changes.
- Evocatively articulates what is inviolable and of central importance to the organization – it has to express what is at the very *core* of the organization that motivates, guides, and constrains how it conducts business.

Realizing these attributes is a tall order. To get at an answer, let's briefly explore the ways in which firms have traditionally been defined.

CONVENTIONAL DEFINITIONS OF FIRMS

There are several ways in which firms are conventionally defined. For instance, definitions could involve boundaries that circumscribe their operations; traditional concepts of business strategy such as the product-market-technology combination; the industries in which they function; the organizational form or structure; and concepts of business or mission.

Boundaries: The boundaries of the firm can be set in practical or theoretical ways. Practical approaches may be as simple as specifying the products to be sold, the likely customers, and the distribution channels. For example: "The firm assembles modular, solar-powered greenhouses for sale directly to homeowners and small businesses in the tri-state region around Pittsburgh, Pennsylvania." Theoretical approaches used by an economist may employ transaction costs[2] to determine the boundaries of the firm. Or a strategy professional may employ the criteria of substitutability of supply and substitutability of demand[3] to define the boundaries. The resulting statements will certainly be replicable by others, but do not necessarily lead to unique and valuable insights

Boundaries, though a meaningful description, have considerable drawbacks. Outsourcing and alliances make the organization's boundaries porous and nebulous. Also, they tend to constrain the organization within the space defined by the boundaries. In a changing world, they stifle the organization's critically important ability to grow and transform. They confuse and constrain rather than inspire.

Traditional concepts of business strategy: The traditional product-market-technology (PMT) statement of strategy is quite similar to the statements derived from the organization's boundaries, though in this case they explicitly add the technology employed to link the firm's product or service to the selected market segment. The constraining influence of PMT statements is quite strong and results in the firm tending to have blinders on about disruptive technologies. They tend to moor the firm to its existing business model, while the forces of globalization, innovation, and shared value demand that the firm initiate quantum changes.

Industries: To define the firm by the industry in which it operates is a dodgy approach in today's world. If a firm, a few years ago, had chosen to define itself as being a manufacturer in the "telephone industry," it would probably be non-existent today. Even if it had successfully made the leap to being a manufacturer in the "cellphone industry," it would face a dismaying challenge in defining the industry in which it functioned. Would it be phones, digital music players, GPS devices, cameras, video cameras, organizers, gaming, computers, or communications? Perhaps, the firm is in the mobile Internet-access industry? At the moment, this last definition of the industry might appear to make the most sense. But who knows what tomorrow will bring? Businesses today experience an explosion of industry obsolescence, convergence, and disintermediation that punctuates and complicates the historical, gradual evolution of industries.

Even if the industry does not experience disruption, goals oriented towards sustainability and growth often motivate diversification out of the industry. For instance, PPG, which began as a manufacturer of glass, soon abandoned its original name of Pittsburgh Plate Glass and shifted to PPG because it entered other industries such as chemicals and coatings (paints). PPG's entry into the chemicals business was driven by its need to control its material supplies for the glass business, a move that major glass businesses around the world – such as Saint-Gobain in France and Asahi in Japan – found to be necessary. Moving from chemicals to coatings was a small step to an adjacent business. Today, PPG's primary source of profits and growth is its global architectural and automotive coatings business, more so than its initial glass or chemicals businesses.

And even in supposedly stable business contexts, firms still often have to reposition themselves very differently within the same "industry." One instructive example, at a more granular level, is PPG's "automotive replacement glass" (ARG) unit. ARG produced and sold replacement glass (windshields, and rear and side windows) for automobiles. Facing severe price competition from Chinese manufacturers, this unit redefined itself as a "logistics" company that also manufactured glass, abandoning its decades-old concept of business as a "low-cost manufacturer" of replacement glass for automobiles. By developing its logistics capability, PPG shifted the competitive arena from price to service. The company worked to ensure that any one of its more than 20,000 installers across the country would be able to access replacement windshields for any make or model of car within one hour. The mission of ARG changed from a focus on producing replacement windshields and car windows to a focus on logistics capabilities and differentiation in customer service. Instead of manufacturing all the replacement glass that it sold, PPG accessed products from any source of supply, including, of course, from the reduced, in-house manufacturing capability that it retained.

It is worth noting that though this repositioning stood PPG in good stead for some years, new competitive pressures forced PPG to add new capabilities such as information technology (IT) in order to respond to an aggressive domestic competitor named Safelite Group Inc. Safelite set up a system that networked with insurance companies. Safelite verified customer claims, replaced windshields, and then invoiced the partnering insurance companies. This reduced the size of the claims departments in insurance companies, which is estimated to have saved them as much as $100 per claim. PPG's vaunted logistics-based service was potentially no longer a competitive advantage for the 70 percent of replacement windshields that were paid for by the insurance companies. In order to stay competitive, PPG had to develop a new competency founded on IT.

In this sense, PPG actually made lemonade from the lemons that its competitors served up. PPG's corporate level invested in and further developed the new competencies that its ARG unit had developed in order to remain competitive. Logistics and IT units were created at the corporate level, and new personnel with relevant expertise were recruited. A new position of vice president for IT – with a corner office no less – was created, and an experienced individual was recruited for the position. PPG's C-suite recognized the relevance of these new competencies to its other glass units and, insightfully, also to the chemicals and coatings units. Networking with its customers and suppliers was supported by the IT capability, embodied in a new corporate-wide system known as Lynx. Logistics capabilities also proved to be valuable in the other businesses. In PPG's paints for residences, for example, distribution was more significant than raw materials in the cost structure. Logistics capabilities were, therefore, a major source of competitive advantage, supporting both cost leadership and differentiation strategies.

This little tale has several morals. First, of course, is the lesson that defining the firm's business is a challenge and possibly could become a millstone that prevents the firm from responding to change effectively. Second, responding to change necessitates developing new competencies. The third moral is that if the firm meets this challenge with resolution and resourcefulness, it can create capabilities and a *Weltanschauung* that will exploit and embrace change and transformation. These are points that we will enlarge upon later in this chapter.

Organizational transformation and shifting industry contexts tend to go hand in hand. IBM famously is no longer a mainframe computer company focused primarily on the United States. It has given up even the personal computer business that extended its focus beyond mainframes, and which it once dominated. It is now more of a global consulting company that relies primarily on knowledge, analytics, and networking – not on design, engineering, manufacturing, and large electronic computing devices.

There are structured approaches to defining the firm's industry, which unfortunately are not really helpful in the face of the three mega-forces. Economists may be inclined to force-fit the firm into one of the codes offered by classifications such as the SIC (the US government's traditional classification scheme) and NAICS (North American Industry Classification System, which is employed by business and government agencies). Such definitions are meaningless from the strategist's point of view, because the focus of strategy development should be on situationally defined, coherent, and discrete subsets or segments of an industry. An industry as a whole would fall into the realm of the industrial organization economist, not the strategist. The point ultimately, however, is that defining the firm on the basis of its "industry" has little strategic meaning in a changing world where the lines between the industries are continually blurring and in flux.

Organizational form or structure: To define a firm as functionally organized (U-form), or multi-divisional (M-form), or as an acquisitive conglomerate is a snapshot[4] that may or may not hold in a changing business context. In the feed-forward framework developed in chapter 5, a modular, evolving organization was seen as capable of exploiting disruptive technologies, co-creating value, and responding to wicked problems.

Indeed, organizational structures or forms are no longer viewed as permanent or long-lasting. In more stable times, in the twentieth century, organizational forms that were borrowed from the Catholic Church and the military served as the template employed by most organizations and were presumed to be long-standing, if not permanent. They are close cousins to the unjustly maligned bureaucratic form of organization credited to Weber.[5] Bureaucracy is a highly efficient form of organization in stable and relatively simple contexts. However, such contexts are hard to find today, leading to the nearly universal disenchantment with bureaucratic forms of organization. Today, organizations such as Honeywell and Royal Dutch Shell view their structures as variables to be manipulated in the search for higher performance.[6] Novel organizational forms such as clusters[7] are designed to be flexible. In short, today, organizational structures are dynamic and responsive to both changing strategies and changing environments. We will explore these dynamic organization forms in greater detail in chapter 8, which looks at modular structures as a component of the feed-forward framework.

Concept of business or mission: In practice, the mission statement and definitions of the business tend to focus, as traditional strategy does, on elements such as products, markets, and technology (PMT). Abell,[8] for instance, in one of the better-known works on defining the business, suggests that business definitions should include three dimensions (which just happen to map onto the PMT definition of strategy):

- Served customer functions (i.e., products/services)
- Served customer groups (i.e., markets)
- Technologies used (i.e., technology)

While this view of how to define the business does possess the enduring, distinctive, and core/central characteristics that we seek in a statement of identity, it still provides us with only a glimmer of what we need. There is some promise in what mission statements are supposed to be. They are intended to be an expression of the purpose of the firm, its raison d'être. The raison d'être of the firm, with its inherently enduring character, could serve as an element of the identity construct that we are engaged in developing.

DEVELOPING THE ORGANIZATIONAL IDENTITY

We are in search of what is core, enduring, and distinctive about a firm. These are the characteristics of the concept of "identity,"[9] which has been gaining much traction in the management literature. There are three elements in firms that possess the characteristics that we are seeking: (1) the *values* embraced by the organization, (2) the *aspirations*[10] that are espoused, and (3) the *competencies*[11] it possesses. They all relate to and indeed drive the formation of strategy. They are not necessarily constrained by the blinders that accompany commitment to an industry. They can transcend discontinuities and disruptions with continued meaning and relevance. Each of these three elements is discussed below.

Values: It has been asserted that firms are founded on a "logic of values"[12] and that values are of "sublime importance."[13] Values, it can therefore be argued, inform and perhaps even determine the raison d'être of firms.

Values can directly impact the strategy of the firm. Values determine the relative importance that the organization ascribes to its various stakeholders. Consider the three most commonly discussed stakeholders:[14] shareholders, customers, and employees.

The importance given to these three classes of stakeholders is a strategic choice that the firm's leadership has to make.[15] This choice significantly impacts the organization's strategy and performance. Of late, there has been growing recognition of the importance of employees in the quest to maximize profits. Both practitioners[16] and academics[17] have described and explained how and why a focus on employees leads to both higher profits and greater sustainability. Employees possess vital tacit knowledge that cannot be codified in manuals or included in databases. Consequently, the firm's source of sustainable competitive advantage probably resides with its employees. Stanford University professor Jeffrey Pfeffer[18] adds a human dimension to the discussion by presenting the emotional and physical toll of layoffs and downsizing. The dysfunctional mix of survivor's guilt and damaged morale that accompanies layoffs has an inevitable, negative impact on profits.

The importance given to each of these stakeholders actually does depend substantially on the values espoused by the firm. Milton Friedman[19] argues, for instance, that it is unethical for a firm not to give primacy, if not sole importance, to shareholders. Dean of Harvard College and Harvard Business School professor Rakesh Khurana,[20] by contrast, makes a powerful argument that giving primacy, if not sole attention, to shareholder value delegitimizes management as a profession. Khurana argues that "it was only after a sustained quest for social and moral legitimacy – finally achieved through the linkage of management and managerial authority to existing institutions viewed as dedicated to the common good – that management successfully defined its image as a trustworthy steward of economic resources represented by the large, publicly held corporation."[21] Values determine whose philosophy the firm adopts.

Who is right is not important to this discussion. What is important is to recognize that values impact strategy, and that this impact happens regardless of the industry in which the firm operates. Values are at the core of the organization. Values transcend disruptions. Values can have a guiding influence on strategy and performance in other ways. Values can determine whether a firm employs criteria such as environmental sustainability, gender equality, diversity, integrity, quality, and safety in choosing between strategic alternatives. Strategies that align with these humane criteria have an impact on the firm's performance. There is a growing body of research and a broadening acceptance by managers of the importance of these humane values and their positive impact on both the bottom line and economic sustainability.[22] They are prime candidates for adoption by firms as guiding the way in which they do business and in promoting synergy between social and economic benefits.

Aspirations: This is the second constituent element of the proposed identity. Cyert and March's[23] seminal work on the behavioral theory of the firm provides a great perspective on aspirations. They demonstrated that a higher degree of stretch or reach in an organization's aspirations can motivate a more concerted search for innovative alternatives, hence affecting the organization's strategy. This affirms the earlier assertions about the positive impact of stretch goals and BHAGs on innovation, which have been discussed in chapters 2 and 5.

As articulated by Freeman, Harrison, and Wicks,[24] a firm has a responsibility towards multiple stakeholders, and its aspirations should encompass goals beyond profits. And as we noted earlier, Khurana[25] (2007) makes a powerful argument that giving sole attention to shareholder value delegitimizes management as a profession. Also, the response to shared value requires a commitment to multiple goals. At the simplest level, the "balanced scorecard,"[26] which has achieved wide recognition and acceptance, suggests that, in addition to shareholder-oriented financial goals, the firm needs to address goals that are responsive to the customer, that relate to processes and productivity, and that reflect the firm's growth and innovation. This set of goals will certainly color the organization's strategy. In addition to recognizing stakeholders other than shareholders, the balanced scorecard approach does make an important point, namely, that the firm needs to seek to improve the performance of the existing business and simultaneously seek to exploit innovations that could lead to new businesses. Wicked Strategies need to meet both of these goals – the improvement of the existing business and the growth into new businesses.

The transformational growth that Wicked Strategies seek, also requires goals that are not constrained by the past. For instance, market share, which is perhaps the most widely employed measure of strategic performance and competitive strength, may not be suitable for incorporation in the organizational identity. Market share is substantially a historically oriented measure in that it refers to a historical conception of the market. It focuses management attention on traditional definitions of the market rather than motivating managers to anticipate, embrace, and stimulate disruptive change. An alternative, enduring goal derived from a desired future would be, for instance, the proportion of revenues and profits that come from new markets each reporting period.

In short, the Wicked Strategies approach requires its aspirations to incorporate:

- Multiple goals responding to the priorities of significant stake-holders,
- Future (vision)-derived goals that motivate the firm to embrace change, and
- Stretch or reach goals that push performance beyond the existing business.

Competencies: This is the third element of the identity construct. The importance and lasting nature of competencies has been brought home by the growing emphasis on the resource-based view of the organization.[27] There have been several dissertations honing the concept of competencies. For instance, the notion of sustainable competitive advantages,[28] such as the ability to learn faster than the competition, has been proposed. The business-process-oriented variation of competency that has been labeled "capabilities"[29] has also gained much attention. But, the most compelling and widely accepted concept related to competency is that of core competency proposed by Prahalad and Hamel.[30] While there is great value and appeal to the idea of core competency, the approach to competencies that is proposed in the context of identity is significantly different from the popular understanding of core competency.

While Prahalad and Hamel do recognize that a firm possesses multiple competencies, their thesis is that a core competency leads to the development of multiple products. For instance, Sharp Corporation's development of and command over LCD technology led to efficient, solar-powered calculators, organizers (PDAs), televisions, and camcorders with innovative LCD viewfinders. Honda Motor Company's core competency in internal combustion engines has led to a plethora of products, including portable power generators, lawnmowers, motorcycles, and automobiles. So we go from a core competency to multiple products.

For identity to support Wicked Strategies, what is needed is an array of competencies, not just a core competency or core competencies. This array of competencies has to be mutually supportive. For instance, in the case of Walmart, its enormous success is built on an array of competencies that are strongly linked. This is quite obvious when one looks at Walmart's strengths and advantages in logistics, supply chain, RFID (radio-frequency identification) technology, IT, cost control, and merchandising. There is no single core competency that is the basis of Walmart's success. It is the synergistic combination of these competencies that has made Walmart the company with the largest revenues in history.

An array of competencies enables a firm to go beyond adjacent products or markets in the search for growth and increased profits. Chakravarthy and Lorange[31] convincingly argue that both growing existing businesses and entering new markets are necessary for profitable growth. An array of competencies offers more points of leverage for entering new markets. In addition, entering new markets will require the development of new competencies. The conventional wisdom regarding competencies is presented in figure 6.1, whereas the approach to competencies in the context of Wicked Strategies is presented in figure 6.2.

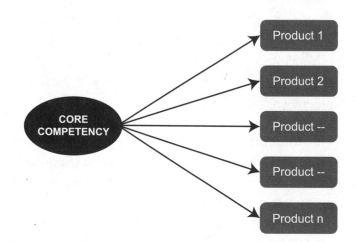

Figure 6.1 Conventional Approach to Competencies

Examples can be found of companies that, over time, tend towards the Wicked Strategies approach to competencies. Google is a good example. From its original expressly held focus on search as its core competency and the core of its businesses, it has moved into a variety of businesses – self-driving cars, smart thermostats, human longevity – that demand a growing array of competencies

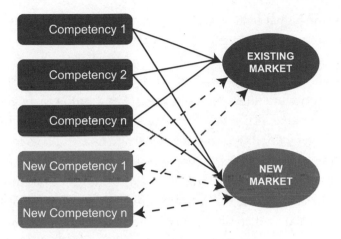

Figure 6.2 Wicked Strategies Approach to Competencies

related to its search and data analytical strengths. Asahi Glass's foray into electronics is a powerful example of nurturing new (electronics technology) competencies that could then be brought to bear on its core-business-related new ventures into high-tech glass with advanced functionalities such as varying electrical resistance and selective transparency.

In the Wicked Strategies approach, transformative growth and profitability are sought through the avenue of new markets. If the firm possesses an array of interlinked competencies, it increases the likelihood that the firm can find competencies that it can leverage to support its entry into new and distant markets. The new markets may require the development of new competencies[32] that are added to its array. These newly developed competencies may also prove to be a source of competitive advantage for the existing markets.

To recapitulate, the construct of identity, which is one of the three components of the feed-forward framework for Wicked Strategies, is intended to capture and articulate what is core, enduring, and distinctive about the firm. The *values* that the firm espouses are at its core, the high *aspirations* that it embraces are enduring in character, and its array of interlinked *competencies* is what makes the firm distinctive.

The values, aspirations, and competencies that constitute a firm's identity are intended to illuminate and guide management's decision making. The way strategies are made real is through developing, evaluating, and selecting strategic initiatives for implementation, and through the resource allocation process. There are effective methodologies for translating the values, aspirations, and competencies embodied in a firm's identity into a decision framework. A formal well-communicated decision framework can ensure that managers act consistently, and that they align with the firm's identity when evaluating and prioritizing strategic initiatives, and directing resource allocation. In chapter 9, I will present proven, widely employed techniques which have been found to be very effective in creating a decision framework that employs the firm's *identity* to motivate and strategically align its actions and programs.

The second component of the framework – feed-forward – is explored in chapter 7, which follows.

CHAPTER 7

Feed-Forward: Framing the Future

Without leaps of imagination or dreaming, we lose the excitement of possibilities. Dreaming, after all, is a form of planning.

Gloria Steinem

Feed-forward is the second constituent of the feed-forward framework. Traditional planning and control systems rely substantially on feedback – which means learning from experience and analyzing actual performance in relation to planned performance. Disruptive technologies and wicked problems delink the future from the past, making traditional systems inadequate. The new models that result from co-creation of value could make the disconnection even greater. Feed-forward[1] processes and techniques address the disconnect that exists from the past by guiding management[2] in making choices today by working back from an anticipated or desired future, without necessarily relying on past experience.

While similar planning and control techniques may be employed in feedback as well as feed-forward approaches, there are profound differences between the two. Feedback is basically an exercise in remediation; correcting, learning from, and improving upon performance in an existing business, while feed-forward focuses on fashioning a future – a future that may be unrelated to the past – that the firm wishes to see happen. Feedback essentially involves performance appraisal and learning, while feed-forward focuses on managing uncertainty and an unknowable future. Feedback continuously improves managerial decision making by advancing the understanding of cause–effect relationships, while feed-forward involves a leap of faith, committing to a belief in a cause–effect relationship in order to make strategic decisions and allocate resources. Feedback-oriented systems engage in episodic reviews of performance at specified intervals of time – say, monthly, quarterly or yearly, while feed-forward-oriented systems trigger analysis whenever assumptions that have been made appear to be mistaken and new issues are spotted. Feedback employs databases that collect historical data, while feed-forward works with information and insights derived from possible future scenarios. In short, feedback analyzes the past and feed-forward strives to envision and realize a desired future.

These differences are summarized in table 7.1.

Table 7.1 Feedback and Feed-Forward

	System	
Characteristic	Feed-forward	Feedback
Purpose	Fashioning the future	Remediation
Focus	Managing uncertainty and an unknowable future	Performance appraisal and learning
Ethos	Committing to an assumed cause–effect relationship	Improving known cause–effect relationships
Trigger	Emerging issues (continuous)	Time period (episodic)
Information base	Predominantly future (possible scenarios)	Primarily past (historical data)
Analytical orientation	Visioning	Past performance

Designing and implementing feed-forward processes is not a simple task. In this chapter we will offer planning and control processes and guidelines that should make the design and implementation of feed-forward easier.

The primary planning technique that supports feed-forward is scenario building. There are multiple approaches to scenario building.[3] We will describe two powerful *scenario-building approaches* that support feed-forward – "possibility scenarios" coupled with robust actions, and "transformational scenarios" linked with enablers. These two approaches respond to two different and challenging *kinds of uncertainty* in the environment. A pragmatic taxonomy and description of different *types of uncertainty* will therefore be presented first to enable selection of the appropriate scenario-building process.

This chapter will also provide a perspective on important *human resource practices* that are aligned with and support feed-forward in organizations. Finally, guidelines for supporting organizational transformation and building the feed-forward vision and business model will be derived from industry experience.

TYPES OF UNCERTAINTY

Courtney, Kirkland, and Viguerie[4] offer a taxonomy of four kinds of uncertainty that is helpful in matching the various scenario-building approaches to the context. In my practice, I have found that the taxonomy is powerful and relevant, but I have over the years refined and simplified it, and I will be employing my simplified understanding in guiding the design of feed-forward processes in this chapter. The figures in this section map onto my simplified version of the taxonomy.

The four kinds of uncertainty defined by Courtney, Kirkland, and Viguerie are characterized by the following circumstances: volatility around a point estimate; the presence of multiple, different futures; the likelihood of a wide range of possible outcomes; and widespread, chaotic ambiguity.

The first kind of uncertainty, *volatility around a predicted end point* (figure 7.1), is akin to projecting sales revenue or profits, and specifying, with a certain level of confidence, the range within which the actual sales or profits may fall. For this kind of uncertainty, *predictive* scenario building describes the likely future, with pessimistic and optimistic variations. Detailed programs or action plans are developed for the likely scenario and contingency plans are developed for pessimistic and optimistic scenarios. This approach is aligned with classic planning processes, and ties in with a feedback-oriented approach, where the future is predicted based on an understanding of the past.

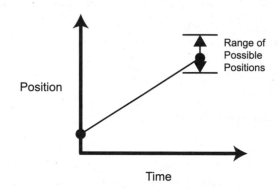

Figure 7.1 Type 1 Uncertainty: Volatility around a Singular Projected End Point

Predictive scenarios are widely employed, and most firms are familiar with their development and use. Also, as indicated earlier, predictive scenarios are more feedback-based than feed-forward-oriented. For these reasons, we will not be exploring predictive scenario building any further.

Coming back to the taxonomy of uncertainty, it bears noting that, as the atomic physicist Niels Bohr is reputed to have said, "Prediction is very difficult, especially about the future." The second kind of uncertainty, *multiple different futures,* bears out Bohr's aphorism. In many contexts a single end point with some predictable volatility doesn't exist. Disruptive technologies and government regulation can create alternative, very different futures.

A graphic example is the impact of regulatory changes on US industries such as health care (the regulations relating to "Obama Care"), financial services (the Dodd-Frank regulations), utilities (controls on pollution and greenhouse gas emissions), nuclear power (safety regulations) and communication (governmental spectrum management and frequency-band allocations). This kind of uncertainty (figure 7.2) is generated by the challenges – disruptive technologies, conflicted stakeholders, and wicked problems – created by the interactions of the three mega-forces.

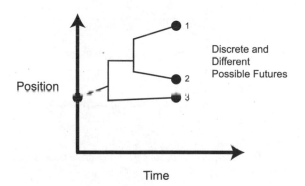

Figure 7.2 Type 2 Uncertainty: Multiple Different Futures

Possibility or *learning* scenarios[5] are capable of coping with multiple alternative futures. This scenario-building technique helps identify *robust actions* that can reasonably be expected to work in all the alternative futures that may happen. Possibility scenarios and robust actions are useful feed-forward techniques and will be described in detail later in this chapter.

The third kind of uncertainty occurs when there is a future in which the outcomes could span a *wide range of possibilities* (figure 7.3). For example, it is possible that the market for the $6000 car that Ford is developing may only be a couple of hundred thousand units or could possibly be as high as several million. This kind of uncertainty can be converted to the previous kind of uncertainty: multiple alternative futures. This can be done by chunking the wide range into several smaller ranges – say, 200,000 to 500,000 units; 501,000 to 1,000,000 units; and 1,000,001 to 2,500,000 (figure 7.4). The use of possibility scenarios and robust actions is enabled by converting a wide range of outcomes into multiple, smaller, discrete ranges of outcomes,

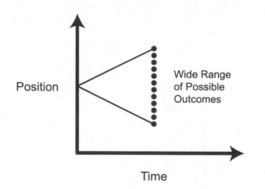

Figure 7.3 Type 3 Uncertainty: Wide Range of Possible Outcomes

The fourth and final kind of uncertainty (figure 7.5), *chaotic ambiguity*, relates to a situation in which there is a total lack of clarity about what the future may be like. Here the cliché that "the best way to predict the future is to create it" comes into its own. *Transformational* or *visionary* scenario approaches may be the only path forward in the face of chaotic ambiguity. These scenarios lead to the identification and deployment of *"enablers"* that help the firm to transform itself and realize its vision. Building and employing transformational scenarios is a great example of a feed-forward-oriented technique.

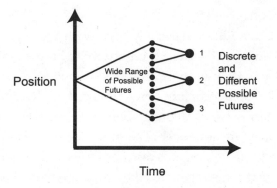

Figure 7.4 Converting Type 3 Uncertainty to Type 2 Uncertainty

The use of transformational scenarios will be further explored later in this chapter.

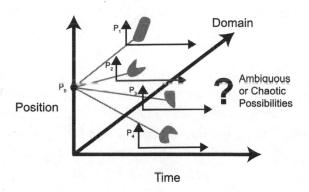

Figure 7.5 Type 4 Uncertainty: Ambiguous or Chaotic Outcomes

POSSIBILITY SCENARIOS AND ROBUST ACTIONS

Conventional, classic *predictive* scenarios seek to forecast and describe the likely future that the firm will encounter. *Possibility* scenarios are markedly different. Possibility scenarios are designed to cope with multiple different futures (Type 2 uncertainty) and with a wide range of possible outcomes (Type 3 uncertainty). Bear in mind that Type 3 uncertainty can readily and usefully be converted to Type 2 uncertainty as illustrated in figure 7.4. The process of developing possibility scenarios starts with the identification of key uncertainties that can impact the future. These uncertainties are employed to describe alternative futures/scenarios that may emerge. For each of the scenarios, strategies and action plans are developed. The strategies and related actions that are common to all the scenarios can then be identified. These strategies and actions that are common to all the scenarios constitute the robust set which can immediately be implemented. The environment is then continuously scanned for indications or signals about which, if any, of the possible scenarios that were identified is likely to happen. When it is clear that a particular scenario is emerging, the firm can then confidently invest in the comprehensive set of strategies and actions that were developed earlier for this scenario.

Some examples should help clarify the process. The current (2015) healthcare situation in the United States, with the ongoing lawsuit regarding subsidies offered through the federal rather than state exchanges; the executive action taken by President Obama relating to the Affordable Care Act ("ObamaCare"); the pragmatic modifications made to ObamaCare during the course of implementation; the modifications imposed by the Supreme Court rulings, with the possibility of more modifications to come; the NGOs' and state legislatures' attempts to influence the healthcare choices for women; the breakthroughs in medical technology and new drugs; and the changing attitudes of the US population – all combine to create an abundance of possible but unpredictable futures for the healthcare industry. In the case of ObamaCare, two key uncertainties that capture or reflect the aforementioned factors mentioned are:

- the level of competition among providers of healthcare, as the size and economics of the healthcare market change, i.e., "provider competition"; and

- the extent to which consumers, rather than employers or government agencies, will be responsible for paying for the services, i.e., "payment shift to consumer."

In juxtaposing two possible states of each of these two uncertainties, as shown in figure 7.6, four *possible* scenarios emerge:

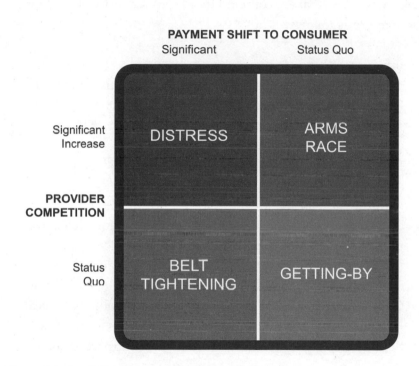

Figure 7.6 Possibility Scenarios: US Health Systems

1 Distress (significant increase in provider competition and significant increase in payment shift to consumer)
2 Arms race (significant increase in provider competition and status quo in payment shift to consumer)

3 Getting by (status quo in provider competition and status quo in payment shift to consumer)
4 Belt tightening (status quo in provider competition and significant increase in payment shift to consumer)

For each of these four scenarios, I have developed detailed strategies and action plans and gone on to examine the sets of strategies for actions that are common to all four scenarios. These robust actions are as follows:

- Building the brand image of the health system. This would reduce the inclination of consumers to shift to competitive providers.
- Providing wide access to measures of the quality of services. This would enhance the brand equity and promote the confidence of consumers in the system.
- Emphasizing customer service. Consumer loyalty would naturally increase as a consequence of excellent service.
- Investing in information technology. Information technology and systems are key to supporting operations, enhancing and tracking quality, and supporting customer service.
- Engaging in research. This would improve the quality of patient outcomes and provide a competitive edge.
- Constraining costs. The ability to charge less would be critical in all contexts and particularly so when patients exercise care in their choices because of the greater financial impact on them.

The power of this approach is evident in the practices of well-managed health systems, such as Boston Medical Center (BMC) and the University of Pittsburgh Medical Center (UPMC), which can be observed implementing the robust actions identified here, in the face of the great uncertainty about which future may emerge. Incidentally, BMC can also be seen making major investments in patient care that are not reimbursed under current regulations, in what can only be described as a "visionary" or "transformative" move. BMC's move may influence regulators and insurance companies to support their initiatives, as the benefits to patient outcomes and patient satisfaction are demonstrated. This visionary/ transformative approach will be discussed later in this chapter, but first I would like to share another example of possibility scenarios and robust actions that convincingly demonstrates the power of the technique.

The US Postal Service (USPS) engaged in developing possibility scenarios and robust actions in the late nineties. This was before the terrorist attacks on 9/11. Why this example is interesting is that even after the consequent economic damage and security-motivated changes in how business and travel are conducted, even after two recessions, and even after the anthrax attack that changed postal procedures, the robust actions developed in the nineties still hold true.

It bears mention that the USPS is a huge organization. It handles 40 percent of the postal traffic in the world. At the time the robust actions were developed, it had approximately a million employees. Also, at that time, the contribution to surplus from first-class mail (letters) was about $1 billion.

The two uncertainties that the USPS believed to be significant were:

1 Electronic diversion. By this is meant the shift from first-class mail/letters to electronic communication such as faxes and email.
2 Pricing flexibility. While the USPS is privatized and receives no subsidies, it is still overseen by the US Postal Regulatory Commission, an agency that has authority over proposed rate changes, mail classification, and major service changes. Within these constraints, the USPS competes with private firms.

The four scenarios that the USPS identified and analyzed are presented in figure 7.7.

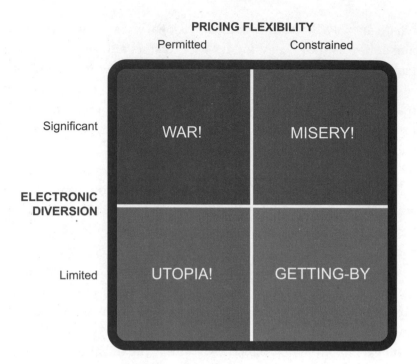

Figure 7.7 Possibility Scenarios: US Postal Service

Analyzing these four very different scenarios leads to the identification of the following "robust actions" that are pertinent to all four scenarios:

- Emphasize automation. The USPS handles an enormous volume of mail – over a third of the total global volume. Economies of scale and related cost reduction can be effectively achieved only through automation. The USPS, though it is not widely known, successfully strives to be on the leading edge of the use of automation to scan, sort, and route first class mail.
- Focus on personnel policies and practices. With close to a million employees then, but down to 620,000 today, formal, intense,

and effective human resource management is essential. The USPS recognizes and seeks to respond to this imperative. The colloquialism "Going Postal," which refers to an employee going berserk and resorting to gun violence in the workplace, is an unfortunate and undeserved attribution. The USPS's statistics show that the proportion of its violent workplace incidents is not out of line with per capita occurrences in other industries.

- Implement tracking. The threat of electronic diversion for letter mail necessitates that the USPS revive the attention it used to pay to package and parcel deliveries as important sources of revenue. In order to do this, the USPS needs to meet customer expectations, which requires real-time tracking capabilities similar to those offered by the wholly private package-delivery industry. The USPS has been implementing and improving this capability. This is an enormous effort that involves training literally hundreds of thousands of employees.
- Stress public relations. With the barrage of criticism that its competitors engage in and the long-standing impression of inefficiency, the USPS has no alternative but to engage in an ongoing and significant public relations effort.
- Develop alternative revenue sources. Enhanced new products and services, such as broad-line postal stores and personalized stamps, and new business ventures, such as warehousing, logistics, and inventory management, are a means of generating the resources necessary to be competitive.

Every one of the robust actions identified over 15 years ago continues to be relevant today. But the complexity and uncertainty that characterizes the environment has not spared the USPS. The major initiatives to venture into new businesses in a quest for additional revenues were scotched by the US Congress. The motivations behind Congress's decision are not clear. Perhaps it is the belief that profitable businesses should be restricted to the private sector.

It is intriguing, though, that the USPS has been placed under severe financial stress because the Postal Accountability and Enhancement Act passed by Congress in 2006 obligates the USPS to fund within ten years all the pension obligations it has incurred! Businesses generally do so only when employees retire, not when the obligation is incurred.

To compound the problem, cost-cutting measures that the USPS has considered to reduce the financial pressures, such as eliminating deliveries of mail on Saturdays, have been vetoed by Congress. At the same time, Congress has limited rate increases for the USPS's most significant service – first-class mail – to the level of inflation.

The uncertainty and complexity faced by the USPS are escalating. The general public is, naturally, against cutting services. Major companies are eyeing or entering the business domains in which the USPS is not allowed to operate. UPS and FedEx, the biggest parcel carriers, will undoubtedly react to the greater competition from the USPS as it seeks to increase revenues by gaining a larger market share in the package delivery business. The USPS had largely given up on aggressively competing in the package delivery business until 9/11, when UPS was hobbled by the terrorist attack on the World Trade Center. At the same time, while competition between them intensifies, both UPS and FedEx are partnering with the USPS to deliver packages that are better suited to the capabilities of the USPS, which, despite all of its travails, still has much greater resources in certain areas than any of its competitors. For instance, the USPS has the largest fleet of vehicles in the world, and has the unique capability to reach every address in the United States every day.

The strategy limitations of the USPS are taking on the dimensions of a wicked problem, with significant stakeholders displaying conflicting priorities. The stakeholder management possibilities are severely constrained because the USPS is not permitted to lobby

Congress, "incentivize" other stakeholders, or reposition itself (see figure 3.1).

But, despite its current sad plight, the USPS story offers an important and inspirational lesson. Every single one of the robust actions identified almost two decades ago remains relevant. The actions may buy the time needed for the USPS to come up with a Wicked Strategy to conquer its current, seemingly overwhelming challenge. The use of the feed-forward framework to develop such a Wicked Strategy will be presented in chapter 9.

TRANSFORMATIONAL SCENARIOS AND ENABLERS

Transformational scenarios offer the promise of coping with chaotic ambiguity (Type 4 uncertainty). They essentially define the vision of what and where the firm wishes to be and identifies the enablers that will help the firm achieve the vision.

The process of developing transformational scenarios and fashioning an implementation plan that focuses on key enablers is a surprisingly simple three-step process. The three steps are:

1 Visualize and describe the *desired future* of the organization and its environment.
2 Identify the *"enablers"* that can bring about or result in the desired future.
3 Develop an *implementation plan* for influencing or acquiring the enablers that can create the desired future.

The example of a graduate school of business provides an illustration of the process. Graduate business education is big business and traditionally has served as a reliable source of cash for universities. But in recent years, graduate business education has descended into turmoil. There has been a proliferation of business schools throughout the world. New players, including the governments of emerging economies and for-profit businesses, have been aggressively entering the arena. Businesses that need management talent are increasingly developing the talent in-house. Some others are shifting from recruiting graduates of master's programs to recruiting individuals with bachelor's degrees. The role and profession of management is being intensely debated. Distinguished academics such as Harvard professor Rakesh Khurana argue that the profession has lost relevance and credibility. Leading CEOs, such as Paul Polman of Unilever, are expressing their support for business models and management philosophies that genuinely and wholeheartedly respond to social and environmental priorities. Others are doubling down on the popular understanding of Milton Friedman's singular focus on profits and the shareholder.

Importantly, disruptive educational and distance-learning technologies are blurring the future and the viability of the vast majority of business schools. Harvard Business School gurus Michael Porter and Clayton Christensen have engaged in public, intense debate about how their school should employ these technologies. The technology challenge is made more complex by the widespread emphasis on live human interactions and experience-based learning as the key to developing leadership skills and effective managers.

And in the midst of this philosophic, pedagogic, technological, and, indeed, existential turmoil, applications to MBA programs have been declining significantly.

In this turbulent context, a hypothetical North American graduate management school may execute the following strategy based on our three-step process: vision, enablers, and implementation. The *vision* expresses the enduring values, aspirations, and competencies of the organization. The *enablers* derive from the vision. Each element of the *implementation plan* is supported by and also reinforces one or more of the enablers. Both the organization and its context are targeted for transformation by the vision and implementation plan. In the context of the graduate school, the synergy of the three elements would look like this:

1 Vision: Become an acknowledged world-class, innovative, management school:
   a. Renowned for a revolutionary, pragmatic, experience-based, career-oriented pedagogical approach that adds high and recognized value to the students' capabilities.
   b. Respected for contributing to management theory and practice with a global perspective and reach.
   c. Prized as an ally that enhances both the economic value and social benefit generated by its partners.
2 Enablers:
   a. Global, sustained media recognition for radical and effective approaches to preparing students, which are advocated and validated by leading executives and academics.
   b. Intense and intimate partnerships with selected, leading, corporate, non-profit, governmental agency, media, and NGO employers of MBA graduates in multiple countries.
3 Implementation plan:
   a. Share the vision, implementation plan, and economic and social sustainability projections with key stakeholders and donors, and build a war chest.
   b. Use the war chest to recruit two or three faculty renowned for both research and consulting, or institutional leadership – public scholars and visionaries of the stature of Paul Krugman, Larry Summers, Michael Porter, Jeffrey Pfeffer, Jeffrey Immelt, Paul Polman, Elon Musk, Gary Hamel, Indra Nooyi, or Clayton Christensen.
   c. Identify and partner with two leading management schools, one in Europe and one in Asia. (In Europe, preferably the

UK, Switzerland, Holland, Denmark, or Norway; and in Asia, preferably in India, so as to reduce language problems.)

d. Build intense and intimate relationships with select and committed corporate, non-profit, governmental agency, media, and NGO partners along the dimensions of:
   - Curriculum and pedagogy development
   - Recruitment and selection of students
   - Scholarships
   - Internships
   - Placement
   - Continuing education
   - Research projects.

e. Design and implement a curriculum that is suited to students with three-plus years of managerial experience, with the following design parameters:
   - Concentrated, three-module, experience-based programs, completed in nine months to a year
   - First two modules to be taken on continents other than the student's home, with the third module on the home continent
   - Second and third modules to follow a cooperative education model, with internships that are technically oriented in the second module and strategically oriented in the third module.

f. Make extensive use of synchronous online education with:
   - An amphitheater-styled classroom in each of the three schools
   - Two large screens (with Cisco TelePresence or equivalent) in each classroom
   - Virtual teams for assignments, drawn from the three locations
   - Best faculty from the three schools.

g. Include selective consulting for corporate, non-profit, governmental agency, media, and NGO partners in the job description of faculty.

There are certain guidelines that can improve the effectiveness of the process. First, the enablers, of course, involve the transformation of the firm, but it must be emphasized that enablers may also involve transforming the business environment. When FedEx began as what was, at that time, the largest startup in history, it created the hub-and-spokes model of operations, and located the hub in centrally positioned, weather-friendly Memphis, both decisions that Art Bass, the then-president, made to create the activity system necessary to achieve Chairman Fred Smith's vision. But FedEx would never have achieved the success it did had it not also transformed the business environment. Fred Smith and Art Bass got the Civil Aeronautics Board's regulations changed to enable FedEx to use large airplanes, replacing the small Falcon 50 jets that it formerly had to use to get access to airports without going through a complex and demanding permitting process. And FedEx had to get USPS regulations changed to enable it to carry certain types of mail.

The second guideline is that transformational scenarios must align with the firm's identity. The identity construct was created to provide strategic guidance for the firm, guidance that would transcend disruptions. Identity provides the platform on which the vision is built. This guideline is diagrammed in figure 7.8.

The outcomes of creating and realizing transformational scenarios are illustrated in figure 7.9. Adjacent opportunities would exist in new businesses in which the key success factors map onto existing competencies, as well as in the improvement of existing businesses by adding new competencies. New businesses that require the firm to develop new competencies would represent a true transformational initiative, involving new business opportunities based on disruptive technologies and transformational business models.

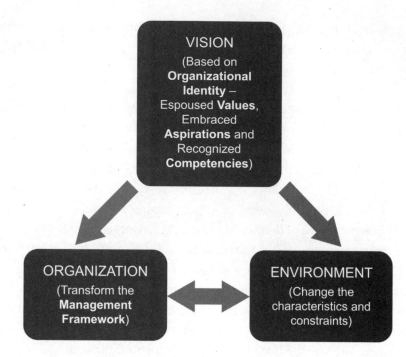

Figure 7.8 Transformation Template

HUMAN RESOURCES FOR FEED-FORWARD

Human resources play a major role in effective feed-forward. The human resources function is viewed as the most important function in countries such as Japan and India.[6] In the context of feed-forward, the importance of the human resources function cannot be overemphasized.[7] Recruitment practices have to ensure that the values of the personnel brought into the firm are aligned with its identity. A combination of recruiting the "best athlete" and of recruiting for specific capabilities to address identified weaknesses or lack of capability within the firm needs to be adopted. The human resource system should be designed to grow employees' capabilities, and so building on a "best athlete" base would

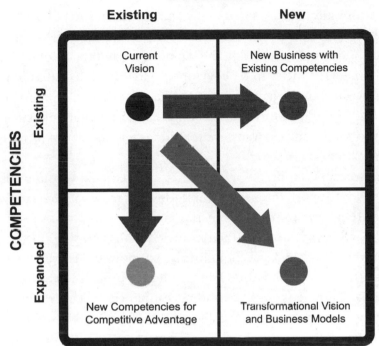

Figure 7.9 Impact of Transformational Initiatives

be an advantage. At the same time, new competencies may be urgently demanded by new businesses that the firm is entering, which may mean recruiting personnel with specific knowledge and skills.

There has to be more than just a willingness on the part of employees to grow their capabilities. There must be a corresponding ongoing process in the firm to add to the knowledge and skills of employees, which supports new competencies that are required by the new businesses and new business models that the firm will constantly seek to develop. In companies such as Merrill Lynch Credit Corporation, which I studied in depth as part of a benchmarking exercise, managers valued the opportunity to develop new capabilities in anticipation of strategic initiatives and new businesses. The managers saw such development as increasing their worth and contribution to the company. Such a mindset and the flexibility that accompanies it need to be developed and supported. It is important because the dynamic modular structure that is the third component of the feed-forward framework requires that personnel be moved across units to transfer capabilities and develop a firm-wide perspective.

Performance appraisal in a feed-forward context would be used more to support the growth and development of the employees rather than to reward and punish.[8] Personnel whose actions and decisions affirm that their values are aligned with the firm's should be cherished and thoughtfully supported. Figure 7.10 indicates the recommended developmental approach related to two criteria: alignment of values and performance. It bears noting that alignment of values is weighted highly. Individuals whose performance falls short but whose values are aligned with those of the organization are supported and provided with development opportunities. By contrast, high performers whose values are not those of the corporation are candidates for outplacement, even if their performance is good. Values are at the core of the organization and behavior that is in conflict with espoused values should not be acceptable.

ENABLING TRANSFORMATION: BUILDING THE FEED-FORWARD VISION AND BUSINESS MODEL

Transformational business models offer the promise of rejuvenating the firm and improving sustainability. In fashioning the vision and disruptive business models that can drive feed-forward (generally) and the transformational scenario process (specifically), a

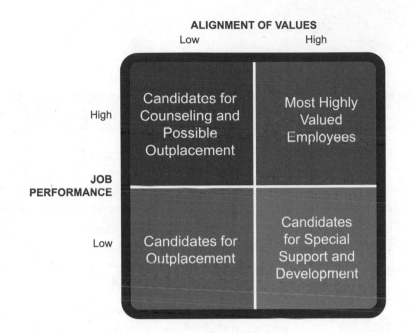

Figure 7.10 Alignment of Values and Job Performance

good starting point is the value chain. Herein, there is a twist that is critically important. Existing elements and processes are rarely the basis for transformation or new business models. It is the changes in the value chain caused by disruptive technologies, new distribution practices, new sources of supply, outsourcing of functions and processes, and so on that indicate the need for and suggest the possibility of new business models. The impact of digital technology on products that previously employed analog technologies is a good example.

For instance, let's examine the value chain for industries based on two fundamental physical phenomena that impact quality of life: light and sound. The imaging and music industries have gone from analog to digital technologies and can effectively illustrate how the business model can be transformed. The basic value chain for both industries can be reduced to the sequence diagrammed in figure 7.11.

Acquisition >>> **Processing** >>> **Storage** >>> **Reproduction**

Figure 7.11 Traditional Imaging and Music Industries Value Chain

Almost everyone today has a digital camera in their purses or pockets, whether it is a standalone camera or the camera function on their smartphones. Film cameras and chemical-based imaging have become more of a curiosity, a niche item like vinyl music records for the few remaining aficionados. Digital imaging has been available for decades, but in the last 15 years its use has exploded. One of the prerequisites for this surge in use of digital cameras is, of course, the constantly reducing cost of the devices. But the dominant reason for digital imaging taking over from classic silver-halide chemical imaging is the changes in the value chain triggered by developments in digital technology, especially the Internet. The transformed value chain is diagrammed in figure 7.12.

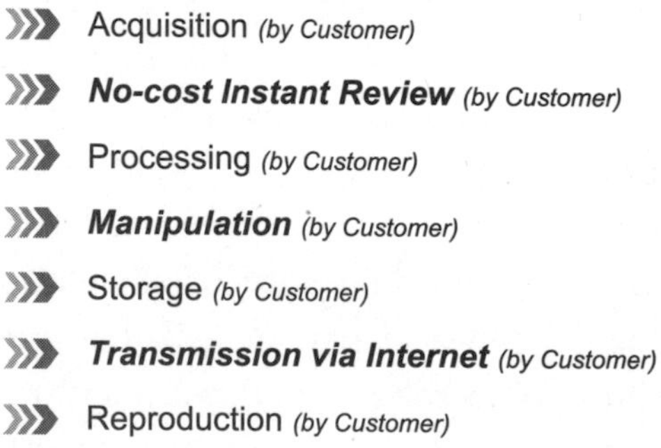

>>> Acquisition *(by Customer)*

>>> *No-cost Instant Review (by Customer)*

>>> Processing *(by Customer)*

>>> *Manipulation (by Customer)*

>>> Storage *(by Customer)*

>>> *Transmission via Internet (by Customer)*

>>> Reproduction *(by Customer)*

Figure 7.12 The Transformed Digital Imaging Value Chain

While the fact that the cost and price of digital cameras have come down from astronomical to manageable levels is certainly a contributing factor, the surge in digital cameras is the result of the additions and changes to the value chain, which are italicized in figure 7.12.

There are several aspects to and consequences of the transformed value chain that have *implications* for visioning and feed-forward. First, the new elements offer disruptive advantages and dramatic new functionality. For example, grandparents can instantly access images of their newborn grandchild from 10,000 miles away. Individuals can add, delete, or modify their presence in images. Millions of copies can be distributed at no cost around the world. And so on. This means that *tremendous added value may be generated by the new functions and benefits. The resulting value proposition offered to the customer has to be specified.*

Second, much lower costs to the customer, compared to traditional imaging, are a consequence of the changes. For instance, an unlimited number of images can be taken at no measurable cost, other than the image maker's time, to find the one perfect image. This change might provide room for higher margins for digital cameras as the total cost may still be lower for customers. *Consequently, the cost–price–demand relationships, that is, the micro-economics of the new value proposition, have to be explored and defined.*

Third, the customer has much greater control over elements of the value chain – both the old and new elements – than ever before. Image editing by the customer and truly instant imaging are now possible. Previously, even Polaroid's brilliant "instant" photographs took a minute or so to develop and were not at all amenable to being edited. But, customer control is a double-edged sword. The value to the customer increases, but the firm may find it difficult to appropriate any returns from the added value provided. *Customers are in the driver's seat. Their perceived rights and unfettered expectations are what should guide the firm's actions. The customer has to consciously recognize that the firm can somehow provide greater value in terms of con-venience, quality, or safety, which warrants ceding some control and shar-ing value with the firm.*

In this situation, partnering with the customer would be highly desirable, enabling the customer to co-create value. Also, systems solu-tions, which simplify the customer's purchasing process and decision, and which provide an optimum, turnkey configuration of products and services, will be desirable if not essential to attract and retain the customer.

Fourth, the new elements in the value chain demand new compe-tencies. Software, electronics, communications technology, and so on are beyond the capabilities of the traditional firms in the photog-raphy (photo-sensitive chemicals and coatings) industry. Develop-ing these competencies, such as software design, may be difficult if not impossible. *If acquiring or developing needed new competencies is not built into the processes and structures of the firm, it will have to seek alliances with firms that possess these competencies.*

Fifth, complementary products and services are necessary to make digital imaging functional. Charge-coupled devices (CCDs, which are the sensors that convert light into digital information), software for image processing, and information storage devices, Internet access, and color printers are complementary products and services that are needed to make digital imaging work. This means that *collaboration not competition should be the focus of the firm. Value added will have to be shared equitably with the providers of these comple-mentary products and services. Again, a systems solution that packages and integrates an optimum (standalone/turnkey) configuration of comple-mentary products and services may be essential in order for the firm to be competitive. It would be desirable for the firm, if possible, to control the most important element in the value chain, so as to maintain the collabora-tion, the "value net,"*[9] *of the "complementors."* For instance, in the digi-tal imaging context, the most important element would be image acquisition – the CCD, the sensor that converts light into electronic signals – as the competencies to handle the other elements (image processing, storage, reproduction, and transmission) of the value chain are readily and widely available.

Similar characteristics and implications are reflected in the music value chain. It is possible, perhaps even likely, that a similar pattern of implications may be encountered whenever disruption impacts a value chain. Be that as it may, it is evident that the changes to a value chain are what should be looked at for guidance in developing a responsive strategy.

A set of value-adding actions that respond to the changes in the value chain can be, if they are aligned and mutually reinforcing, melded into a strategy that exploits the disruption. The firm's identity provides the lens though which the alignment of the actions can be assessed. Such an action-to-strategy sequence, Lindblom's[10] branch-to-root process, is what we determined in chapter 4 to be an effective approach to dealing with wicked problems. This identity-driven process of developing the vision and strategy will be detailed in chapter 9.

Guidelines for Transformational Business Models

Linear thinking and hard-earned insights from past experience are a siren song that is difficult to resist. Organizations have to consciously create the context in which transformational business models can merge. We will identify guidelines for creating such a context by examining the disruptive change that took place in the music industry around the turn of the century.

The behavior of the five music majors – Bertelsmann Group (BMG), EMI, Sony Music Entertainment, Universal/Polygram, and Warner Music Group – in response to the advent of digital technology and the Internet offers a cautionary and educative tale. They clung to their old business model, which essentially revolved around the distribution of physical recordings of music: records, tapes, and CDs. Until the late 1990s, their understanding of the industry value chain was based on a model[11] that originated in the 1930s (figure 7.13). The evolution of the value chain subscribed to by the music industry majors in the mid-nineties is presented in figure 7.14.

| Record Manufacturers 》》 | Record Distributors 》》 | Retail Outlets |

Figure 7.13 Music Industry Majors' Concept of the Value Chain, 1930–95

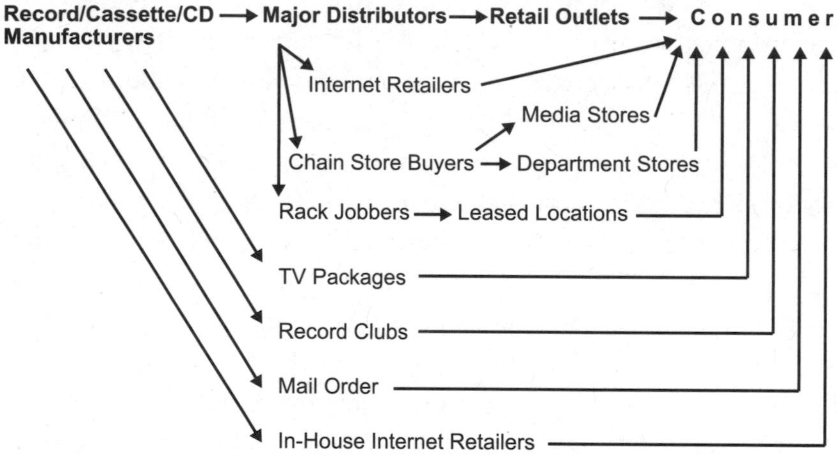

Record/Cassette/CD → **Major Distributors** → **Retail Outlets** → **C o n s u m e r**
Manufacturers

Internet Retailers

Media Stores

Chain Store Buyers → Department Stores

Rack Jobbers → Leased Locations

TV Packages

Record Clubs

Mail Order

In-House Internet Retailers

Figure 7.14 Music Industry Majors' Concept of the Value Chain, Post-1995

The expansion of the distribution channels for the physical recordings of music captured the imagination and attention of the major labels. They were misled into thinking that the explosion of distribution channels was the strategic change to be addressed. They did not see that this was just a difference in degree, not a difference in kind. The difference in kind engendered by digital technology was viewed as a passing threat that could be addressed by non-market moves such as litigation.

Not surprisingly, the major labels viewed the Internet as just another order-taking mechanism. The linear thinking exhibited here led to them attacking and suing potential customers for downloading and "pirating" music. They saw value being lost because of declining sales of records, tapes, and CDs. They were oblivious to the reality that the revenues in the music industry had the potential to increase dramatically because of digital technology. Fifteen downloads of 99¢ tracks earned just as much as a 15-track CD, and cost less to deliver to the customer. Also, customers would buy many more of these tracks because of the ease with which they could be searched for and found, and the instant gratification of downloads.

It took Apple's marvelous "systems solution," combining a well-designed but otherwise undistinguished and typical music player (the iPod) and a website (iTunes) for searching for and downloading individual tracks, to exploit the enormous potential unleashed by digital technology. The great success of the iPod and iTunes combination stemmed substantially from it being designed to meet every consumer expectation – from finding music to flexibility in paying for music

This tale, combined with the lessons suggested by the preceding value-chain discussion, offers us a set of guidelines for taking the transformational leap to a new business model:

- Constantly seek ways to make the current business model obsolete.
- Articulate a value proposition, which includes both economic and societal value.
- Engage in experimentation and make it a practice and priority to analyze "failures," learning from difficulties encountered. ("Fail fast" is the war cry among the converted.)
- Focus intensely on emerging *differences* in the value chain, differences in kind not just in degree.
- Try to control the key element in the emerging value chain; and try to build the competencies necessary to do so in a

timely fashion by training and education, or by acquiring the competency by recruiting qualified personnel.

- Build alliances to gain needed competencies that cannot be readily developed or acquired.
- Recognize and partner with "complementors," ensuring that all earn fair shares in the value generated.
- Link with lead users/customers (connect R&D with customers) to get a sense of their needs and future trends.
- Develop one-stop shops and systems solutions for the customer.
- Break all the rules to respond to the customer.

There are a few final points to be made about feed-forward. Feed-forward, as was mentioned earlier in this chapter, often requires a leap of faith. The business model will have to assume cause–effect relationships that have yet to be demonstrated or proven. It would be unreasonable to expect that every such cause-effect assumption will prove to be valid. Setbacks and failures will occur. Managers and especially the C-suite need to be prepared to take these failures in stride but to also examine whether the logic underlying the assumptions of cause–effect relationships is sound. Managers, paradoxically, have to commit to an untested cause-effect model to the extent of investing resources and unreserved effort into making it work, but at the same time be actively examining if the cause-effect model is valid. This is difficult to do, though utterly necessary.

Some years ago, when I had the occasion to speak with the top management of Fujitsu, I asked them how and when they determined that a strategic initiative or major project was a failure. They patiently explained that my question had no meaning in the Fujitsu context. In Fujitsu, when initiatives or projects did not progress as planned, management's focus was on what needed to be done differently, not on labeling the initiative and the responsible managers as failures. Similarly, in a feed-forward context, well-planned and thoughtfully implemented initiatives are *experiments* that provide a better understanding of cause–effect relationships and underlying assumptions.

Feed-forward is inherently inclined to render existing value propositions and business models obsolete. This is not a bad thing if the firm at the same time strives to keep the existing business going until it is evident that the emerging business model dominates. A flexible and dynamic approach to the firm's organizational structure will be needed to execute this complex balancing act well. The design of such dynamic structures is taken up next in chapter 8.

CHAPTER 8

Modular Structure: Supporting Transformation

You can't force creatives into a box. If you try, they'll no longer be creative. And no one will want your box.

Ryan Lilly

Modular structure is the third component of the feed-forward framework. In chapter 5, we determined that the fundamental objectives that modular structures have to meet are to stimulate and support the firm's development of new businesses that (1) embrace disruptive technologies and new business models; (2) enable and enhance the performance of the existing businesses in the firm; and (3) develop and deploy new competencies needed for the new businesses.

Organizational modules that serve the first two objectives – relating to new and to existing businesses – have existed for some time. There are a host of examples of these two modules, so we will only describe them briefly. However, the third module intended to develop new competencies is not formally incorporated in firms in the manner needed to support Wicked Strategies, so we will describe this module in some detail.

Before describing the modules, a simple typology of organizational structures may be helpful. Conventional organizational structures were captured in Greiner's classic model of organizational growth.[1] Greiner's directive or functional form is the "division" subunit level in figure 8.1. The "collaborative" or multi-divisional form is represented by each "group." Greiner's "coordinating" or conglomerate organization is the "corporate" level in figure 8.1.

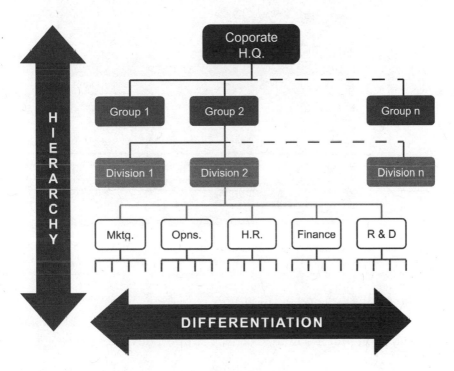

Figure 8.1 Traditional Organizational Structure

The two dimensions that define the classic organizational forms represented in figure 8.2 are the horizontal dimension of specialization or "differentiation," and the vertical dimension of "hierarchy." These two dimensions create the matrix presented in figure 8.2. The organizational units that are identified in the matrix provide a focus for our discussion.

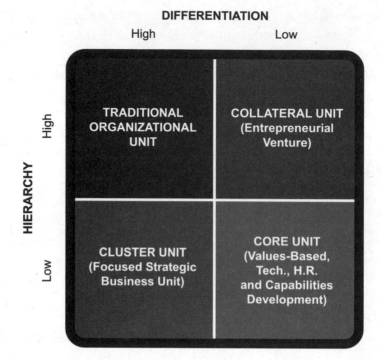

Figure 8.2 Alternative Organizational Modules

The traditional organization unit is high on hierarchy and differentiation, just as it is diagrammed in figure 8.1. This traditional organization unit has little to offer in support of Wicked Strategies.

MODULE TO STIMULATE AND SUPPORT NEW BUSINESSES

Collateral units that are high on hierarchy and low on differentiation are typical of Lockheed Martin's Skunk Works division for advanced research, which was described in chapter 3 in our discussion of co-creation of value. These units are essentially project teams and act as powerful engines of innovation.

At first glance, it may appear that a skunk works is low on hierarchy and high on differentiation, but this is not the case. Project leaders are usually given the authority to choose and change the members of the team. Even self-managed "super teams"[2] have a corporate sponsor who constitutes and provides resources for the super team. Therefore, a hierarchy in terms of power exists, even if this reality is not readily obvious.

Furthermore, these skunk works and project teams endeavor to limit the differentiation that exists in the unit. Lawrence and Lorsch's classic work[3] on differentiation (and integration) identifies four dimensions along which differentiation exists: *goals, interpersonal relationships, structure,* and *time.* Members of project teams, though they have been brought on board because they possess the necessary diversity of skills and knowledge, are necessarily similar on these four dimensions of differentiation. Consider some examples in which all members of the team or skunk works have the same *goal*: to build a car that can seat four and be sold for $2000 (Tata Nano); to build a spy plane that can fly above the reach of surface-to-air missiles or fighter jets (Lockheed U-2); or to provide honest, reliable, and inexpensive money transfer services to low-income people who do not have bank accounts (Vodafone M-Pesa). The ways members of the teams are expected to interact with one another is explicitly specified, making for homogeneous *interpersonal relationships.* The *structure* dimension does not come into play as all team members belong to the same unit. And all are committed to the same *time* frame to achieve the unit's goals.

The collateral units are initiated as start-ups, assigned with the mission of commercializing an idea or disruptive technology and growing it into a sustainable business. In time, these collateral units either become stable businesses or are unsuccessful and are disbanded. If the unit is disbanded or sold, personnel in the collateral unit revert to the core unit (as described below), and are retrained or re-educated before assignment to another collateral unit or cluster unit. If and when collateral units become stable businesses, they may then be managed as cluster units with emphasis on profits, investment in sustaining rather than disruptive innovations in technology, employment of specialized capabilities organized into subunits or departments, and focus on a defined set of customers.

Disruptive technologies, co-creation of value, and wicked problems, as we have seen, all give rise to new business models and new businesses. These collateral units that support innovation and are unconstrained by the existing business's mindset would be a valuable module serving an important role in the firm's organizational structure, if the firm intends to develop and deploy Wicked Strategies.

MODULE TO ENABLE AND ENHANCE EXISTING BUSINESSES

Cluster units have been described in helpful detail by Mills.[4] They align very well with the original concept of strategic business units (SBUs). SBUs are autonomous, profit-making units of firms, which have a strategy that is distinct and different from other SBUs in the firm. SBUs have a unique charter or vision, they utilize a unique product-market-technology combination, and they face a unique set of competitors.

The characteristics of cluster units, as described by Mills, contribute to the effectiveness of SBUs. Traditional profit centers require a variety of specialized capabilities and, because they are relatively stable, are formed from departments or subunits, which tend to be silos of knowledge, disciplines, and expertise that do not integrate very well. Clusters, as conceived by Mills, emphasize the common vision or charter, focus the attention of all members of the cluster on the customer, and encourage connections and shared responsibility between the disciplines, individuals, and subunits in the cluster. They are consciously low in hierarchy and high on specialization, but have formal processes to ensure connections across the silos that specialization engenders. Cluster units possess characteristics that support ongoing businesses and are a necessary module to include in the structure of the firm.

These two modules are analogous to the key constituents of what have been labeled ambidextrous organizations.[5] The first module, which is designed to stimulate and support new businesses, is similar to the revolutionary or exploration-oriented component of ambidextrous organizations. The second module, which is intended to enable and enhance the performance of the existing businesses, is similar to the evolutionary or exploitation-oriented component of ambidextrous organizations. The third module, which I describe below, creates a modular structure different from that of ambidextrous organizations.

MODULE TO DEVELOP AND DEPLOY NEW COMPETENCIES

While cluster units (strategic business units) and collateral units (entrepreneurial ventures) are commonly encountered in business organizations, core units laser focused on developing the organization's new competencies are hard to find. In his discussion on cluster-based organizations, Mills[6] describes core units as the home of the leadership, of the top management. While the core unit under development here will also include the leadership of the firm, it is much more than that. Every employee of the firm belongs permanently to the core and is seconded to the cluster and collateral units. They may return to the core unit for retraining, education, and development when needed, or when the cluster or collateral unit to which they have been seconded is terminated or sold.

The core unit is primarily a competence-development unit engaged in R&D and in the development of human resources. The dominant subunits in the core unit focus on a competency or a set of related competencies. Many firms have such subunits. PPG's logistics and IT units at the headquarters are examples mentioned earlier.

Perhaps the most important component of the core unit is human resources. After all, competencies reside in personnel. The human resources function is responsible for ensuring that the firm possesses the competencies needed to succeed in new markets by recruiting or developing the right personnel.[7]

The strategic importance of human resources was conveyed to me by Don Beall when he was the chairman and CEO of Rockwell Industries and had gained the reputation of being the most sought-after manager in the aerospace industry.[8] When describing how he was transforming the company[9] he emphasized that Rockwell's VP of human resources was as much or more responsible for effecting the transformation of Rockwell as the VP of finance and strategic planning.

There are three tenets that are of prime importance in the human resources arena. First, the firm has to ensure, to the fullest extent possible, that the values articulated in its identity are genuinely subscribed to by all employees. When recruiting personnel, a firm must make alignment with and commitment to its values an essential requirement.

Second, the firm has to eschew layoffs. In normal circumstances, the only personnel that may be outplaced are those whose values turn out to be unaligned with the firm. Pfeffer's description of the negative impact of layoffs on the bottom line of the firm has been persuasively presented in both an academic article[10] and in a *Newsweek* cover story.[11] The impact on morale is deep and long lasting. Personnel remaining in the firm after others are laid off are known to experience survivor's guilt. Many "survivors" will seek to leave the firm for situations they expect will provide them with more security. And it is inevitable that those finding employment elsewhere will be the best of those that the firm has chosen to retain, resulting in a loss of important capabilities.

Third, the firm has to ensure that competencies are shared across the organization. GE and Rockwell Industries, for instance, are known to transfer personnel from high-tech growth units to less innovative and stable units to rejuvenate them. Sharp Corporation grew and prospered by leveraging counter-conventional niche technologies, and by engaging in a process that the company calls "chemicalization." This involved moving the top 3 percent of researchers to new departments every year. Sharp also engaged in the practice, alien to most Japanese companies, of adding talent drawn from other companies at all levels of the organization, in addition to developing its existing personnel.

DYNAMIC MODULAR STRUCTURE

To recap, the three structural modules that enable firms to cope with mega-forces and lead to the creation of Wicked Strategies are:

1 *Collateral units* that house entrepreneurial ventures, which help a firm to embrace disruptive technologies, enter new markets, and build new business models.
2 *Cluster units* that act as SBUs and effectively manage existing, relatively stable businesses.
3 The *core unit* that develops and strengthens the array of competencies that the firm needs for existing and new businesses, and that in turn enables the firm to retain employees who had been seconded to cluster or collateral units that are terminated or sold.

The collateral and cluster units, particularly the former, enable the firm to readily modify its structure. The collateral units enable the firm to more easily shed the shackles of the existing businesses. And the core unit develops and readies the organization's capacity

to add new collateral organizations. The modular structure is diagrammed in figure 8.3.

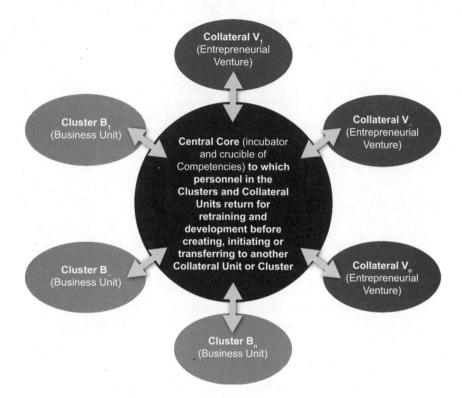

Figure 8.3 Dynamic Modular Structure

The modular structure cannot function in isolation. It needs the
organizational identity – values, aspirations, and competencies –
to give it direction and purpose. The values espoused by the firm
guide recruiting and the retention of employees to populate the
modular structure as it evolves. The aspirations, especially stretch
goals, motivate the formation and functioning of collateral units.
The array of competencies identified as existing and necessary

direct the focus of the core unit. Feed-forward is needed to plan and control performance of the collateral units; feedback is of little value when the unit is focused on developing disruptive business models. Also, robust actions shape the operations of the collateral unit. These are just a taste of the interdependencies that exist between identity, feed-forward, and modular structure.

The demanding but inspirational process of melding these three components of the feed-forward framework to forge and implement Wicked Strategies is the focus of our next chapter, chapter 9.

PART 3

CREATING AND DEPLOYING THE FEED-FORWARD FRAMEWORK

Forging Wicked Strategies: Crafting the Feed-Forward Framework

We shape our buildings; thereafter they shape us.

Winston Churchill

So, we come now to our final task – pulling together the three components of the feed-forward framework that we developed. Let's recapitulate the journey to this point.

First, we started with recognizing the pervasive presence and intrusive impact of three mega-forces – *globalization, innovation,* and *shared value* – on firms. Second, we identified the consequences of the interactions between these mega-forces, recognizing *disruptive technologies, conflicted stakeholders,* and *unknowable futures,* which combine to spawn *wicked problems.* Third, we explored the logical responses that firms can adopt when dealing with the complex and uncertain environment caused by these interactions; and we discerned the *opportunity* for **innovative business models** in disruptive technologies, the *possibility* of **co-creation of value** by conflicted stakeholders, and a *response* to the challenge of unknowable futures in **feed-forward processes.** Fourth, we analyzed the universe of actions that firms could take to build innovative business models, to promote co-creation of value, and to adopt feed-forward systems, coming up with the three constructs of *identity, feed-forward,* and *modular structure.* Finally, we detailed the content, the processes, and the structures that shape these constructs individually and are now ready to explore the feed-forward framework that connects these constructs and serves to formulate and implement Wicked Strategies.

ORGANIZATIONAL ARCHITECTURE FOR WICKED STRATEGIES

The three components of the feed-forward framework – identity, feed-forward, and modular structure – developed in chapter 5 are interactive. Each of the three components of the framework is linked with, influences, and is impacted by the others. The framework diagrammed in chapter 5 is reproduced in figure 9.1.

Though the connections between the components of the framework are interactive, in order to simplify the discussion we will address the connections in a linear sequence. The driving force and foundation of the feed-forward framework is the organizational identity. It provides the stimulus for creative thinking and the screen that will aid in prioritizing the possibilities. The values, aspirations, and competencies that constitute the firm's identity provide the stimulus and establish the screen. The first connection that we will examine in this chapter is between identity and feed-forward; subsequently we will consider the links between feed-forward and modular structure; and then we will complete the linear progression, taking it back to the start by looking at the link between modular structure and identity.

LINKING IDENTITY AND FEED-FORWARD

There is a story that relates well to the link between identity and feed-forward, and retelling it is more instructive (and less

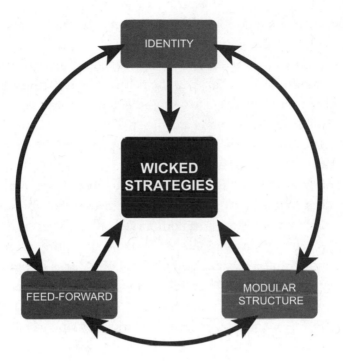

Figure 9.1 The Feed-Forward Framework

demanding) than providing a sterile description of the connection. The story is that of Marks and Spencer, the quintessential British retailer. The firm was founded by Michael Marks, an immigrant from a Polish family who came to England by way of Belarus. Michael Marks received an initial loan (variously estimated as between £5 and £300) from an accountant by the name of Thomas Spencer – hence the name of the firm. Starting from selling merchandise stored in a cart that was wheeled to village markets, Marks and Spencer rapidly grew into the largest British retailer and the largest retailer in the world in the mid-twentieth century.

The critical incident around which this story revolves happened with Michael Marks's son and successor, the first Baron Marks of Broughton. For a Polish immigrant's son to be made a peer of the realm speaks of the economic success of Marks and Spencer, and the fond regard in which it is held by the people and government of the United Kingdom. Lord Marks, at the helm of the brilliantly successful company, one day came to a crossroads in the way he managed Marks and Spencer. He made a choice to run the company the way his father had: hands on, without the complex planning, reporting, and control systems on which large companies typically rely. He had come to realize what, to him, were the most important things in life. Lord Marks's priorities were expressed as two fundamental values: first and foremost, promoting the well-being or *happiness* of the firm's primary stakeholders, and second, accepting *simplicity* as an essential virtue. The stakeholders that Lord Marks recognized, in order of priority, were employees, suppliers, and customers. Notably, shareholders did not make it to the top three! The tightly knit board and top management team – Marks and Spencer like most British companies of the day had a board consisting of operating executives – designed the strategy and operations of the company around these two values. Their approach is presented in figure 9.2.

Committing to *simplicity* as the way to do business led to a limited use of management information systems and a great reliance on "personal probing," as it was called, by management. On any given day, every Marks and Spencer store in the United Kingdom could expect to be visited and queried by two or three executives from headquarters. This paucity of formal management systems meant that the company had to depend on highly competent, knowledgeable, and dedicated personnel. Fortunately, management's values regarding its employees – generous compensation practices and assured job security – led to the workforce being exceptionally loyal.

The importance placed on employees' *happiness* affected the firm's operations at all levels. It shaped the structure of the firm. Every store had two managers of equal stature, one for merchandising and the other for taking care of personnel. Because most of the sales

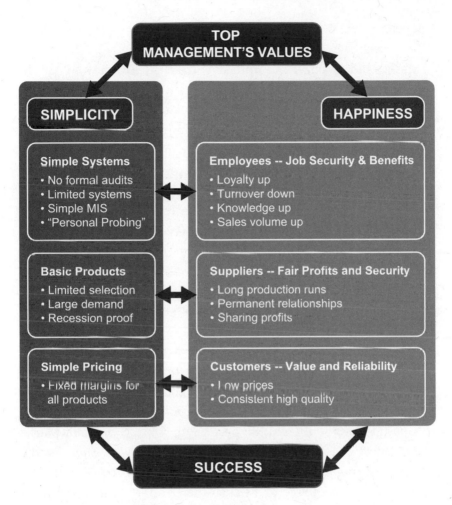

Figure 9.2 Marks and Spencer: From Values to Strategy and Operations

staff were women, the personnel manager usually was a woman. Beyond compensation and job security, the management's intense and close attention to the well-being of employees led to their providing podiatrists for the employees, recognizing that salespeople were on their feet the whole day and consequently tended to suffer from foot problems. The staff was served the same food in the canteens as the directors. Being mostly women, the staff was also given access to beauty salons.

Marks and Spencer's emphasis on *simplicity* showed up in the product line. The company focused on a limited line of basic, recession-proof clothing and food products of the highest quality. The limited product line, which was accompanied by high volumes, enabled the suppliers – all British companies – to ensure quality and reduce costs, resulting in products of extremely high value. The importance that was given to the well-being of suppliers was just as intense and thoughtful as that accorded to the employees. It was not unheard of for a supplier to receive a visit from its Marks and Spencer liaison team (who kept close tabs on design, quality, and production costs) with the message "We need to rework our contract with you. We are not paying you enough." In the context of the typical company's relationship with contract manufacturers, such an interaction would appear surreal.

Marks and Spencer's pricing policy was *simplicity* itself – a fixed markup over costs for every item. No complex pricing models, shadow pricing, or estimations of price elasticity existed. The customer could be assured of a quality product; not necessarily the cheapest, but undoubtedly the best value. On top of it all, Marks and Spencer's clothing was worn and its food was eaten by the board, ensuring that they were totally familiar with the quality, design, and value offered to the customer. And in those days Marks and Spencer specified no time limit within which returns were to be made. This was a company that was "one with the customers," both metaphorically and literally. Marks and Spencer's customers were happy customers.

The Shaping Power of Values

There are several lessons here. First, for our purposes, is the fact that values, though they are intangible, can have a very tangible and direct impact at all levels of the organization. In Marks and Spencer, values drove the following elements at the company:

- Strategy: Choosing to focus on basic products, British markets, and the minimal use of technology (PMT).
- Structure: The engaged, operating role of top management, and the practice of having dual store managers.
- Systems: The simplified planning, reporting, and control practices, and generous compensation and benefits packages.
- Style: Enhancing the well-being of multiple stakeholders – treating employees as family, emphasis on sharing value equitably with suppliers, and focusing on providing unparalleled value and total satisfaction to the customer.
- Policies: Offering unconstrained customer returns, generous personnel benefits, and thoughtful and generous supplier relations.
- Tactics: Using stable and established contract manufacturing, and simple and low pricing.
- Operational: Focus on personal probing, and being immensely thoughtful and caring towards employees.

The Shaping Power and Constraints of Aspirations and Competencies

Marks and Spencer provides us with a perspective on the power of *values* and how they can shape a company and its future. Marks and Spencer also provides us with a perspective on *aspirations* and *competencies*. We will not dwell at length on these, because unlike values, the power of aspirations in the sense of a vision or stretch goals, and the importance of competencies as a foundation of strategy, are well known and accepted. We will focus on aspects of aspirations and competencies that tie up with feed-forward systems.

Celebrating and living its *values* resulted in Marks and Spencer becoming, for a long period, the largest and most successful retailer in history. It saturated the British market. At one time it commanded 60 percent of the British market for ladies' underwear. With *aspirations* to grow, it expanded into Canada with an acquisition. Not surprisingly, this was a total disaster, because Marks and Spencer lacked the *competencies* to operate internationally. Its management was not "one with the customers" in Canada. Personal probing across the Atlantic and across a country 40 times the size of the United Kingdom was impossible. With formal management information systems lacking, there was no way that the Canadian operations could be managed from the United Kingdom, nor could the Canadian operations benefit from the British-focused knowledge that existed in the senior management ranks and board of Marks and Spencer. Furthermore, Marks and Spencer's supply chain was British and could not easily support the Canadian operations. The lack of *competencies* that was required for international operations should have been obvious – but it wasn't.

The lesson here is that formal recognition of the firm's array of *competencies* must be developed and compared to the competencies needed to address the key success factors characterizing new markets. Credible plans to develop the competencies that the firm lacks are a prerequisite to new market or new business entry.

Creative applications of existing *competencies* to new business possibilities need to be explored. In the case of Marks and Spencer, the company had, by operating with integrity for over a century, gained the trust of the people in the United Kingdom. Trust is a key success factor in the financial services industry, and Marks and Spencer's astute entry into financial services and banking has been a success.

There is yet another lesson to be drawn from the Marks and Spencer story. The *competencies* that Marks and Spencer had developed over several decades were peculiarly relevant to a country isolated from globalization. With the development of global supply chains, which met quality expectations at a fraction of the cost of British manufacturers, and merchandising that reflected global fashion trends rather than the traditional styles embraced by Marks and Spencer, competitors made life difficult for the company. Its existing *competencies* were no longer adequate for it to succeed in its traditional home market. Staying with its strategy and its existing *competencies* was no longer a viable approach. This lesson was also learned by PPG's automotive replacement glass business, which, as we discussed earlier, had to keep developing new *competencies* – logistics and IT – in order to remain viable.

There is a subtle point with regard to profit goals or *aspirations* that merits attention. Even though Marks and Spencer's shareholders were not given the highest priority, they did very well. The motivated and competent employees served the customers well, which resulted in excellent value added for the shareholders. This is a commonly encountered phenomenon. For instance, Vodafone CZ places profits at the fourth level in its hierarchy of goals, but it still is a very profitable operation. The reason for this seemingly paradoxical situation is that setting profit goals without identifying the enablers is not helpful. By focusing on the value proposition and, in particular, on the enablers of profit, such as supreme customer service in the case of Vodafone CZ and utterly reliable and highest-value products in the case of Marks and Spencer, reliably leads to the growth of profits.

We are now positioned to explore some of the linkage mechanisms and processes for connecting identity with feed-forward. There are two significant ways in which identity and feed-forward can be linked. These are:

1 Creating a template or profile for assessing the fit between strategies developed by feed-forward and the elements of identity. This technique is labeled *dimensions of strategic choice*.
2 Employing *multi-criteria decision models* that employ values, aspirations, and competencies as the criteria with which to evaluate strategic initiatives.

Dimensions of Strategic Choice

This approach to linking identity with feed-forward is a visual device that received an award from the Foundation for Administrative Research as the most significant contribution to "corporate and organizational planning" in 1983. Despite being developed three decades ago, it continues to be a useful approach. An example of the application of this methodology is perhaps the best way to communicate it.

Consider the example of an organization in the health arena, which opted to remain anonymous in a case study written about it, in which it adopted the name Metrohealth.[1] When engaged in a strategic planning exercise the top management and the board found themselves faced with a values-laden choice. The choice was whether or not to provide healthcare to patients who did not have the personal resources or insurance to pay for the service. This is a choice that most health organizations in the United States face, but often sidestep, or try to ignore.

When analyzing the issue, the organization realized that this choice would impact other important choices that defined its strategic positioning or profile. The four other critical choices that would be decided by this fundamental choice of "type of client" to be served included:

- Revenue sources – to be tapped by Metrohealth, either in the form of insurance companies or a greater reliance on philanthropic sources for support
- Diversification posture – to aggressively seek diversification opportunities into new arenas or be satisfied with the scope of the current business
- Technology posture – to develop or adopt leading-edge technologies or employ technology that is proven and affordable
- Growth orientation – to choose to emphasize rapid growth or resolve to grow to the extent that philanthropic support allows

The board was split on the issue, with the business executives on the board tending to favor one position, and the board's medical professionals, clergy, and social workers tending to take the opposite view. Finally, it was difficult for the board to formally choose not to provide healthcare to anyone who needed it, because most of them were of the view that healthcare is a fundamental human right. The consequences of this fundamental, values-driven choice are indicated by the arrows connecting the dimensions of strategic choice in figure 9.3.

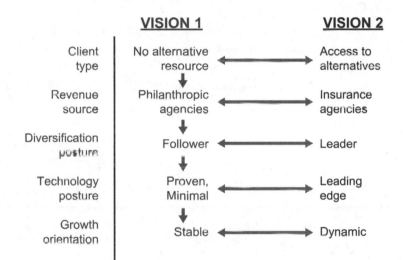

Figure 9.3 Dimensions of Strategic Choice: Metrohealth Example

Examples abound of both types of health organizations – that is, those choosing to serve anybody needing healthcare and those choosing to focus on clients who can ensure the organization's continued economic viability and independence. Creating a profile along key strategic dimensions can serve as a screen or template against which to test the actions and programs generated by feed-forward. If they violate the values the firm has chosen to espouse, they need to be discarded or modified.

The dimensions of strategic choice approach illustrated above is more powerful than the popular "strategy canvas" approach to profiling strategy. An example of a strategy canvas for the business school discussed in chapter 7 is presented in figure 9.4. While the strategy canvas approach may seem similar in appearance to the dimensions of strategic choice, which is the approach advocated here, it does not explicitly assess the logical or practical consistency of the organization's choices across the various dimensions.

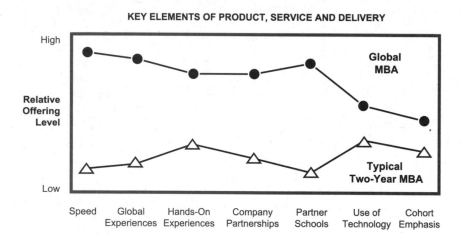

Figure 9.4 Strategy Canvas: Business School Example

Multi-Criteria Decision Models

More structured approaches can be adopted, employing multi-criteria decision models to link the actions and programs generated by feed-forward with the values, aspirations, and competencies defined in the firm's identity. Strategic initiatives, as identified by feed-forward through possibility scenarios and value-chain analysis, can be prioritized by employing these decision models. The values, aspirations, and competencies that form identity would serve as the criteria employed in the decision model. For these decision models, qualitative criteria, and judgments are perfectly functional and acceptable. Even if the strategic initiatives are extremely different in character – for example, some being technical-efficiency enhancements and others being risky startups in a new country – the decision models identified below have been proven to work.

There is a widely employed decision tool based on a methodology called the analytic hierarchy process (AHP) that responds well to the complex characteristics of these choices. It has been embraced by the management of major corporations such as IBM and 3M; agencies such as NASA and HUD; and by governments of major countries such as China and Indonesia. I have used it for over two decades now in a wide variety of situations. I have used it to help companies decide, among other things, which countries are best suited to their aspirations for global growth, which new product possibilities to invest in, which product lines to drop, and which values and competencies are the most significant. The decision itself is obviously helpful, but the process which is employed to arrive at the decision is also of great value. The process helps to both share and to inform the understanding and priorities of participants in the decision process.

Decision software packages (e.g., Expert Choice, and Super Decisions) are available from different vendors. A package incorporating this tool, which offers a free version (http://www.superdecisions. com), is available on the web. These software packages make the use of this powerful tool very simple. The software enables participants in the decision-making exercise to engage in a process of sharing their views to arrive at a consensus understanding of the relative weight to be given to criteria such as the firm's values, aspirations, and competencies. The weights are derived from making a sequence of simple comparisons between two measures at a time, regarding how important each is to making progress towards the overall goal or vision of the organization.

The AHP software allows for the weighted criteria to be applied to alternatives and strategic initiatives. The relative contribution that each strategic initiative makes towards realizing the vision is calculated by the software. Importantly, the software programs enable sensitivity analyses and implicitly offer guidance about how the initiatives can be redesigned to increase their effectiveness.

A hypothetical matrix generated as the outcome of this decision technology is illustrated in table 9.1.

The software programs offer the power of sensitivity analyses that instantly enable changing the relative weights of the criteria, and comprehending visually how robust the priorities of the alternatives are. The software is powerful and flexible enough to respond readily to changes in the environment and to new information gained when implementing the strategic initiatives.

The Advantages of Aligning Feed-Forward with Identity

Feed-forward needs the stimulation and the guidance that identity can provide. In a world of uncertainty and complexity, feed-forward analyses need an anchor to provide a sense of self and place, a beacon to provide direction, and also a chart to point out the rocks, shoals, and dangerous currents along the way. The organizational identity provides all three. Values identify the boundaries of acceptable strategic initiatives and provide constancy though disruptions. Aspirations are the beacon that motivate action and stimulate creativity. Competencies determine the feasible route to take. Either or both methods – the dimensions of strategic choice template or the multi-criteria decision model – of linking identity to feed-forward will provide valuable and useful guidance.

Table 9.1 Illustrative Priority Matrix of Strategic Initiatives (relative contribution of initiatives to the goal of "profitable progress toward becoming the global technology leader in selected sectors")

| Initiatives | Criteria | | | | | Overall score (max: 1.00) |
	Cash flow impact (weight: 0.26)	Sustainability index (weight: 0.15)	H.R. capability (weight: 0.12)	Technology enhancement (weight: 0.25)	Growth (weight: 0.22)	
Equity affiliates in BRIC markets	High	Medium	Strong	Significant	High	0.98 Rank 1
Outsource IT functions	Marginal	Medium	Strong	Negligible	Medium	0.46 Rank 6
Install high-efficiency filters in older plants	Negative	High	Limited	Moderate	Low	0.67 Rank 5
Accelerate shift to green energy	High	High	Limited	Significant	Medium	0.84 Rank 3
Acquire South African operation	High	High	Limited	Negligible	High	0.87 Rank 2
Invest in research to reduce minimum efficient scale	Moderate	High	Strong	Significant	Medium	0.75 Rank 4
Revise service agreements	Moderate	Low	Poor	Negligible	Low	0.37 Rank 7

While we have been looking at alignment as a unidirectional phenomenon from identity to feed-forward, it can also be a two-way street. Feed-forward analyses may come up with possibilities that lead to firms changing their aspirations. New possibilities may motivate the development of new competencies. In extreme cases, it is possible to conceive of a future that may warrant a change in the firm's value system. For instance, values that are based on religious tenets may have to give way to more humanistic values as social mores, government regulations, and laws change. Whatever the directionality, effective Wicked Strategies will require that these two components are aligned.

LINKING FEED-FORWARD AND MODULAR STRUCTURE

Continuing our linear journey, we come to the connections between feed-forward and modular structure. The influence of feed-forward on modular structures is primarily on the collateral units, secondarily on the core unit, with its tertiary impact on the cluster units.

Let's first consider cluster units. The cluster units, as SBUs responsible for established businesses, will need inputs derived from feed-forward processes and techniques only when they choose to rethink their business models or encounter issues of a wicked nature. Established businesses, while relying primarily on feedback processes, are nevertheless exposed to the three mega-forces and have to be alert and proactive to the need for feed-forward. Aspirations for growth emanating from the organizational identity may also motivate cluster units to tilt their management processes more towards feed-forward.

GE's previous CEO Jack Welch's famous "dyb.com" (Destroy_Your_Business.Com) initiative mandated that every SBU manager in GE develop an Internet-based business model and strategy, which would ensure that what Amazon did to brick-and-mortar bookstores would not happen to any of GE's businesses. He had embraced one of the canons underlying the Wicked Strategies philosophy – to make one's own business model obsolete before the competition does it to you. In order to revamp their business models, every established GE SBU had to adopt a feed-forward approach.

While it can be reasonably argued that cluster units may, depending on the circumstances, tilt towards either feedback or feed-forward, collateral units have no choice but to be dominantly and aggressively feed-forward-oriented. It is in the nature of their being. These are entrepreneurial ventures entering uncharted waters. Feed-forward, with the guidance and stimulation provided by identity, is the source of reason and judgment, and the source of the strategic initiatives that lead to survival and success. Strategic initiatives and the novel business models that are the core of these entrepreneurial ventures are derived from the robust actions and the difference-focused analyses of emerging value chains that are the backbone of feed-forward. The basic decision to set up a collateral unit and to embark on an entrepreneurial adventure is derived from the organizational identity through the medium, the intercession, and the processes of feed-forward.

Feed-forward also has a strong role to play in the context of the core unit. The key success factors in the markets entered by collateral units may require competencies that they do not possess. Feed-forward is the means by which the core unit is alerted to the situation, and it initiates the urgent development or acquisition of the needed competencies. In addition, the multi-criteria decision models discussed earlier can structure the process and inform the decision about the priority and the resources to be accorded to the development of the various needed competencies. New competencies that link well with the existing array and offer the promise of strengthening the competitive advantage of other collateral and cluster units should be given priority.

The effort to add to the array of competencies is initially focused on human resources. It will involve training and education or recruitment. If the competency is too challenging and complex to be developed through the human resources channel, the acquisition of or alliance with a firm possessing the competency are alternatives to be evaluated. Here again, the criteria derived from the firm's identity come into play.

The relationship between feed-forward and modular structure is bidirectional, just as in the case of identity and feed-forward. The collateral units serve as the "experiments" that test the feed-forward assumptions and beliefs about cause–effect relationships. Also, information from a collateral unit about which of several possible scenarios is actually emerging may trigger the investments that feed-forward's real-options approach holds in reserve until there is an acceptable degree of clarity about the future.

LINKING MODULAR STRUCTURE AND IDENTITY

This third linkage takes us back to the starting point – identity. There are two strong connections between modular structure and identity. One is the core unit's development or acquisition of new competencies that need to be added to the array of competencies recognized by the firm's identity. The second connection is the evolution of the firm's aspirations – part of the identity – as a consequence of the performance and the possibilities demonstrated by the collateral and cluster units. Aspirations may also be affected by the value-creating potential that can be accessed by the new competencies that the firm may acquire because of the efforts of the core unit.

It is useful to consider creating a matrix that documents the array of competencies and how they might reinforce each other. An example of such a matrix is presented in table 9.2.

The matrix in table 9.2 suggests that among the new competencies to develop, the more valuable ones are in new store formats and

Table 9.2 Competency Relationships

Competencies	Existing					New		
	Logistics	Supply chain	Merchandising	Fleet management	New store formats	Acquisitions	RFID	Government relations
Logistics								
Supply chain								
Merchandising								
Fleet management								
New store formats								
Acquisitions								
RFID								
Government relations								

Legend:

☐ Little or no connection

▨ Mutually reinforcing

■ Strong synergy

RFID because of the many connections between them and the other competencies. Priorities could also be determined with a more structured approach by employing the multi-criteria decision framework.

FORGING WICKED STRATEGIES

The three components of the feed-forward framework, when connected, create a reactor vessel that engenders Wicked Strategies. They create the conditions necessary for Wicked Strategies to come to life. Identity's *values* defines the space and the boundaries within which Wicked Strategies are to operate, its *aspirations* give Wicked Strategies purpose and direction, and its *competencies* give Wicked Strategies the power and leverage to gain competitive advantage for the firm. Feed-forward generates the options, the action alternatives, and the strategic initiatives from which Wicked Strategies can be formed to support the revolutionary business models that also emanate from feed-forward analyses. Modular structure, finally, gives the firm the flexibility and incentive to embrace and implement transformational Wicked Strategies, while continuing to nurture its established businesses.

Let's take a second look at the juxtaposed Classic and Wicked Strategies (figure 9.5) that were presented at the end of chapter 1. The merits of the proposed Wicked Strategy, as well as the logic underlying it, may be more evident now that we have identified design constructs such as identity.

Let's assume a firm with the following identity:

- Values:
  - *Honor and respond without reservation to the customer's needs.*
  - *Provide employees with a sense of worth, safety, and security, and the ability to lead a comfortable life.*

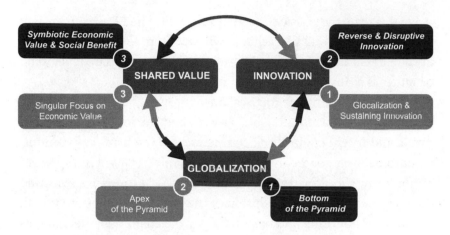

Figure 9.5 Examples of Classic and Wicked Strategies

- *Unfailingly value and reward its shareholders for their trust in the firm.*
- *Be a good citizen and enhance the well-being of the communities in which it makes and sells its products.*
- *Protect the natural environment.*
- Aspirations
  - *To grow profits at a compound annual rate of 12%*
  - *To be the global technology leader in its industry*
  - *To be recognized as an ideal corporate citizen in every country in which it operates*
- Competencies
  - *Efficient low-cost manufacturing that meets the highest quality and safety standards*
  - *Frugal engineering, combining value engineering and lean manufacturing, to consistently reduce costs while improving value to the customer*
  - *Dedicated and experienced workforce*
  - *Experienced and entrepreneurial top management team*

For this firm, the classic strategy does not fit. The 12 percent growth rate that the firm seeks to achieve will not be possible, as the developed markets are stagnant and the apex of the pyramid in developing countries is a tiny fraction of the population.

The Wicked Strategy focuses on a growing market, which is aligned with the aspirations for growth and the low-cost manufacturing and frugal engineering competency of the firm. The commitment to being a good corporate citizen, which is a value espoused by the firm, should ease entry into emerging economies. Meeting the low price points of the bottom of the pyramid is consistent with the value of honoring and responding to the customer's needs. This will further strengthen the frugal engineering and low-cost manufacturing competencies of the firm. It is possible that these enhanced competencies will improve margins and possibly help the firm reach new segments in the developed economies.

The following and final chapter – chapter 10 – presents in detail the application of the feed-forward framework to Walmart, the firm with the highest revenue of any US firm in history.

Deploying Wicked Strategies: Applying the Feed-Forward Framework

Life isn't about finding yourself. Life is about creating yourself.

George Bernard Shaw

Success is not final, failure is not fatal: it is the courage to continue that counts.

Winston S. Churchill

Instead of regretting about the past, what's more important now is to change the present for the future.

Marlon Amparo

To understand the prevalence of wicked problems in the realm of business strategy, there is perhaps no better example than Walmart's situation. Walmart is known around the world for its unparalleled growth and success in the last century. In revenue terms, at $476 billion in 2014, it is the world's largest corporation. To continue its success, as Walmart's shareholders and its management desire, Walmart faces a set of challenges that are difficult to define and grasp. As the largest business organization in the world, with revenues that exceed the GDP of 168 of the 190 countries tracked by the World Bank, the problems Walmart faces are complex and unprecedented.

The many challenges are linked, but the connections between them are hard to perceive and anticipate. Effective responses necessarily involve Walmart engaging with diverse stakeholders in complex ways. To list but a few of the wide-ranging issues faced by Walmart:

- The limited disposable income of its dominant customer segment
- The growing income inequality and declining purchasing capability of minimum-wage workers in its largest market: the United States
- The pressure to increase the wages and benefits of its workers
- The 5–4 US Supreme Court decision on gender discrimination that saved Walmart billions in damages but made it even more despised by NGOs and women
- The need to develop new store formats to tap new pockets of demand in the context of a saturated US market
- Its disappointing entry into fashion garments
- The vexations resulting from its involvement with organic foods
- The drop in growth rates in same-store sales
- The negative reactions of employees, the public, and the government to some of its human resources practices
- The history of community resistance to the location of new stores in urban areas as well as upscale communities in the United States
- The impact of climate change on its products and markets
- The unexpected difficulties experienced by Walmart in Germany, leading to its ultimate retreat from the country
- The unexpectedly smooth entry into Japan but into a dismal economy
- The uncertainties and complexities clouding the attraction to and presumed potential of the BRIC economies
- The identification and gauging of the next generation of "BRIC" economies – such as, possibly, Indonesia, South Africa, and Turkey

- The possibility of tariffs being imposed in response to China's practice of fixing the value of the yuan at an artificially low level and the consequent impact on this critically important source of low-cost goods
- The rapidly increasing wages in China
- The concerns regarding the safety of goods procured from its low-cost suppliers in China
- The widespread and increasing concern about labor conditions in Chinese factories
- The pressures for environmental and social sustainability exerted by NGOs, complicating the imperative of economic sustainability deriving from its shareholders
- The multiple reversals of policies regarding multinational, multi-brand retailers in India, soon to be the country with the world's largest population
- The myriad uncertainties in India, complicated now by the dominance of the new government, in power since 2014 – avowedly business friendly but originating from extreme nationalistic and religious roots
- The unwelcome attentions of aggressive NGOs concerned about Walmart's size, sourcing of products, and human resources practices
- The complex relationship with its Sam's Club subsidiary
- The lack of connection and identity with higher-income consumers
- And so on …

Walmart's problems are many, but is it facing wicked problems? Let's recap the characteristics of wicked problems:

1 The perceived "problem" is unusual and substantially without precedent.

It is without precedent for a retail organization to seek significant growth on a base of $476 billion in fiscal 2014, when it experienced the weakest growth in five years. Even a 5 percent growth rate means that Walmart has to create the equivalent of a Fortune 120 company each year. And Walmart is attempting to achieve this growth mostly from within the confines of a single industry.

Is the problem unprecedented? Yes!

2 There are multiple, significant stakeholders with conflicting values and priorities who are affected by the perceived "problem" or responses to the "problem."

Let's see. Walmart's stakeholders include:

a. Governments across the world with different economic ideologies

b. NGOs that believe that Walmart needs to be reined in

c. Trade unions seeking to unionize Walmart's employees

d. The trade union the Chinese government demanded that Walmart recognize

e. Community activists who perceive Walmart as the source of the vanishing individuality of neighborhoods, the failure of small shopkeepers, the decline of local farms, and the demise of the (upscale) village and main-street aesthetic

f. Environmental activists who see Walmart degrading the environment in a variety of ways

g. Human rights activists who perceive Walmart's sourcing and labor polices as questionable and arguably unethical

h. Low-level employees who seek a "living wage"

i. Employees accustomed to very different cultures – like the German employees who understandably were repelled by the cultish daily morning cheerleading event in its stores

j. Customers who expect Walmart to offer products and services at the lowest price but who are also critical of the cluttered, cost-saving ambiance of its stores

k. Different customer behavior, preferences, and expectations in different countries with different cultures

Do its multiple stakeholders possess conflicting values and priorities? Yes!

3 There are many apparent causes of the "problem" and they are inextricably tangled.

Let's assume for the moment that the "problem" is how to grow profits at a rate that would satisfy shareholders. The limitations to growth and the implications of still seeking growth within Walmart's largest market (the US) include:

a. The saturation of the low-income, price-sensitive consumer segment in the United States, which is served by low-cost sourcing of products from offshore manufacturers

b. The negative reaction of consumers to the dominance of Walmart, who perceive it as "cheapening" the US retail scene, threatening the livelihood of small stores and shopkeepers, and sourcing products from China at the expense of domestic manufacturers

c. The need to develop new, smaller, possibly upscale store formats for locations with higher real estate costs

d. Understanding the needs and motivations of very different customers

e. The inconsistency of the Walmart brand and existing product line with consumers' preferences at upscale locations

f. The need to simultaneously seek growth in other countries

g. Seeking new business models, such as cash-and-carry wholesale, for small shopkeepers in India, where retail sales are constrained or not permitted.

h. Gaining a foothold by servicing wholesale customers who will become competitors and bitter opponents, if Walmart ever enters the huge, growing, almost irresistible Indian retail market

i. Partnering with companies in other markets based on Walmart's competencies (such as cold-chain logistics); partners such as Bharti Enterprises who may eventually turn out to be competitors

j. Major strengths, such as the Walmart brand, its low-cost sourcing, its entry into new markets, and formation of partnerships are interdependent, and are at the same time potential weaknesses.

Do multiple and tangled causes of the "problem" exist? Yes!

4   It is just not possible to be sure when you have the correct or best solution; in other words, no "stopping rule" applies.

a. Walmart's different stakeholders may prefer vastly different "solutions."

b. When entering new markets, Walmart has no way of knowing what the right business model is – value proposition, profit model, activities and capabilities needed; the only way to find out is to experiment.

c. Fundamentally, when the problem definition is clouded, the solutions cannot be anything but unclear.

Is the "no available stopping rule" situation in play? Yes!

5   The understanding of what the "problem" is changes when reviewed in the context of alternative proposed solutions.

a. *Problem*: Growth?

→ *Solution*: New store formats and upscale product lines?

→ *New problem*: Brand image

b. *Problem*: Growth?

 → *Solution*: Entry into BRIC countries?

 → *New problem*: Need to develop new business models and new competencies

c. *Problem*: Growth?

 → *Solution*: Adding financial services?

 → *New problem*: International money transfer regulations

d. *Problem*: Saturated US or Western market; new entanglements with community groups and NGOs; trade/tariff issues; failure to engage effectively with higher-income US consumers; the cultural, institutional and regulatory difficulties of entering the BRIC markets?

 → *Solution*: International growth; engaging NGOs and community groups in co-creating value; partnering with leading retailers in other countries; improved government relations and development of local management talent?

 → *New problems*: Expansion into unfamiliar but large and growing emerging markets, while fighting for market share in familiar developed economies; designing new activity systems and new business models, while refining existing systems and models; creating multiple and complex value propositions; strengthening partners who may eventually become competitors; balancing the interests and addressing the tensions between governments in developed and emerging countries.

Do different solutions change the originally perceived problem? Yes!

Walmart is clearly facing wicked problems. So, how can Wicked Strategies be deployed to help the company continue to grow and prosper? Let's look at Walmart through the lenses and the framework that we have developed.

WALMART AND THE THREE MEGA-FORCES

Walmart has been experiencing the impact of the three mega-forces. *Globalization* is a must for this $476-billion company to grow. Having exhausted the potential for its existing business models, *innovation* is an imperative. Innovation is also necessary to respond to the very different characteristics of markets across the world, especially those in emerging economies. The size and high profile of Walmart and the existence of several adversarial groups – NGOs, labor unions, and upscale communities – demand that it embrace the principle of *shared value*.

Walmart is challenged by the uncertainty and complexity that results from the interactions of the three mega-forces. As we have seen, Walmart is faced with *wicked problems*. The regulatory constraints in countries like China and India demand that it develop *disruptive business models* like cash-and-carry wholesale in India. This business threatens to place Walmart in competition with its current customers at some future date if it ever starts a true retail operation in India. If it entered the retail market, it would have to deal with *disruptive technologies* in packaging, and government-mandated distributed, renewable power generation using DC (direct current) power instead of AC (alternating current) power from the national grid. The Indian government would require Walmart to source 30 percent of its products from India. All these factors require Walmart to develop *innovative business models*. Walmart has had to work with partners in many countries. Especially in India, it worked for years to develop a logistics-oriented business model in partnership with Bharti Enterprises. It clearly has opportunities to *co-create value*.

So Walmart appears to be in the space where, we have argued, Wicked Strategies offer the path to salvation. Perhaps the most extreme situation Walmart faces is in India. Its only current (2015), viable business in India is cash-and carry-wholesale, not retail.

Its much-bruited alliance with Bharti Enterprises to create a badly needed cold chain to get Indian produce to Western tables collapsed in late 2013, after six years of trying. Walmart's hopes have been lifted and dashed with dismaying frequency by the central government. After years of effort, the Indian government passed legislation to allow foreign multi-brand retailers to operate retail stores in India, only to revoke the permission weeks later. A little later, permission was again granted to go ahead, but only in a few southern, more economically advanced states, and with detailed and demanding requirements in terms of local sourcing and sustainable practices. Walmart publicly declared that these demands were too onerous to accept. Then a new government was elected and, with it, Walmart's future seemed to dim even further. The new powerful prime minister, elected with a strong mandate, belonged to a political party that had voiced strong opposition to foreign retailers. A key constituency of this party was the millions of small shopkeepers in India.

A traditional strategic analysis, employing a SWOT (Strengths, Weaknesses, Opportunities, and Threats analysis)[1] matrix based on the facts described above, would probably conclude that entering the Indian market is not justifiable in terms of the bottom line. SWOT analysis is conducted with reference to an existing and accepted strategy – in this case, entering the retail market in India with a traditional, globally sourced line of products. From this perspective, the conclusion is fairly obvious. In the face of so much uncertainty, the rollercoaster of regulatory change, the constraints placed on Walmart, and the open hostility of the political party in power in the central government and in many of the state governments, it appears logical and sensible to bow out of the retail market in India. Walmart decided to do so.

But, what if we employed the feed-forward framework that we have developed? Would that, possibly, change Walmart's decision? Let's first take a stab at Walmart's identity.

Walmart's Identity

Walmart's mission is simple and direct: "We save people money so they can live better." In addition, Walmart's website enlarges on its sense of "global responsibility." It expresses this responsibility through its publicly avowed commitment[2] to:

- Diversity and inclusion
- Building for the future
  - *Recruiting*
  - *Talent development*
- Ethics and integrity
- Safety
  - *Food safety*
  - *Product safety*
  - *Environmental compliance*
  - *Health and safety*
- Responsible sourcing
  - *Empowerment*
  - *Supply chain capacity building*
  - *Worker safety and well-being*
  - *Transparency*
  - *Collaboration*
- Food
  - *Hunger relief*
  - *Healthier foods*
- Opportunity
  - *Women's economic empowerment*
  - *Supplier diversity*
- Community
  - *Disaster relief*
  - *Associate volunteerism*
  - *Local communities*

Walmart's commitment to global, social responsibility finds enthusiastic expression in its efforts to enhance sustainability. What is notable about its efforts here are the collaborations in which Walmart engages. Its five reports[3] in 2014 on sustainability initiatives are all written by its partners, who include companies and NGOs that are environmental activists. The partners are General Mills, Inc., World Wildlife Federation, Shenandoah Growers, Inc., Carbon Disclosure Project, and Plug Power, Inc.

Whether Walmart's commitments to global responsibility are core or peripheral to its being, it is evident, particularly because of its collaborations, that Walmart is taking these commitments seriously. In his introduction to Walmart's 2014 Global Responsibility Report (a link to which is provided in note 3), Doug McMillon, president and CEO of Walmart, makes the commitment personal and heartfelt. Walmart's efforts do appear to be more than just lip service or a concession to public relations. This is reinforced by the reality that Walmart's environmental sustainability initiatives have enhanced its reputation and social sustainability, and also have a significant positive impact on its bottom line and potentially its long-term economic sustainability.[4]

Before hypothesizing a credible identity for Walmart, there is an emerging competency in Walmart, beyond those that are well known and recognized by conventional wisdom. This is its demonstrated capability and impressive record in distributed and green generation of electric power,[5] and its related investment in DC (direct current) power. DC appears to be a disruptive technology that will supplant AC (alternating current) as the form of electric power that will become the standard,[6] certainly throughout the developing world, and, in time, probably also in the developed world.

Drawing from these clues, we can deduce a credible set of values, aspirations and competencies, and from them fashion Walmart's identity:

Values:
- Quality of life of people globally
- Particular responsibility to
  - *Employees who are the future of the company*
  - *Shareholders who have placed their trust in the company*
  - *Customers who look to the company to meet their needs for products and services*
  - *The communities who welcome Walmart as partners with shared interests*
- Responsible global citizenship

Aspirations:
- Grow economic value added faster than the growth in the S&P Index
- Improve the quality of life of people globally
- Become the acknowledged global leader in sustainability
- Be recognized as the most respected and valued company in the world

Competencies:
- Cost reduction
- Global sourcing and supply chain
- Logistics
- Merchandising
- Sustainability practices
- Distributed green power generation

A Multi-Criteria Decision Model for Walmart

From Walmart's identity, a decision model was created employing Expert Choice software. Social responsibility is prominently incorporated in its business model. The criteria, and the weightage for each, were developed using the software. The results are listed below:

1   Economic value added (31.4%)
2   Growth potential (19.9%)
3   Environmental sustainability (9.7%)
4   Fit with existing competencies (8.4%)
5   Resulting and needed new competency development (8.2%)
6   Development of associates (8.1%)
7   Impact on people's quality of life (7.7%)
8   Community well-being (4.2%)
9   Government relations (2.5%)

Economic value added (profit) is clearly the highest priority. The three competency-related criteria – fit with existing competencies, new competency development, and development of associates – when combined equal a score of 24.7 percent, and carry the second-highest priority. The relatively low weight earned by community well-being and government relations was because of the belief that these can best be enhanced by investing in areas such as environmental sustainability and development of employees. Together, however, the three socially oriented criteria – people's quality of life, community well-being, and government relations – carry a significant 13.4 percent of the weight.

Feed-Forward-Based Robust Actions and Business Models for Walmart

To create possibility scenarios and generate robust actions, we need to identify significant uncertainties. Focusing on the Indian context, some of the significant uncertainties include:

• Government regulations affecting foreign multi-brand retail stores
• Entry of other multinational, multi-brand retailers into the Indian market

- The ability to meet the price points of the unorganized sector in India that serves the true bottom of the pyramid – those earning $2 or less a day
- The ability to organize farmers and change centuries-old farming practices to grow safe and organic produce.

Using (1) the uncertainty regarding government regulations and (2) the entry of other multinationals as two dimensions of a matrix, we can create the following four scenarios (figure 10.1).

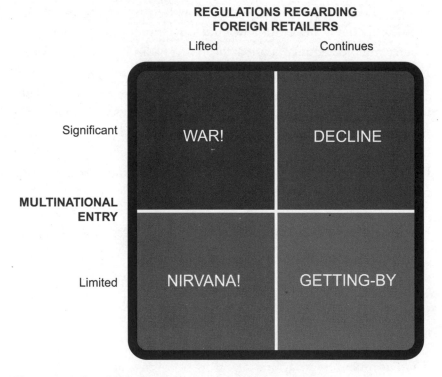

Figure 10.1 Possibility Scenarios for Walmart

Assuming a continued presence in India and then developing the plans for each of the four scenarios, the following *robust actions* and related strategies emerged:

1 Continue existing cash-and-carry wholesale warehouses.
2 Expand products and services to existing wholesale customers.
 – Connect on the Internet via smartphones (16 million cell phones are sold monthly in India, geographic coverage is extensive, messaging is popular, and rates are the lowest in the world) to interact with customers for order taking, prepackaging orders, and information about special sales.
 – Add money transfer services using cell phones (a version of Vodafone's M-Pesa system).
 – Improve products made available to wholesale customers for resale to consumers. It can be accomplished through adding new single-use packaging and achieving lower price points.
 – Develop farming cooperatives for producing organic and high-quality produce. Walmart can provide selected produce to Indian wholesalers.
 – Add products targeting the wholesalers themselves – such as inventory and order management apps, and free-standing solar power and DC lighting systems.[7]
 – Introduce consumer durables for distribution through selected wholesalers to low-income consumers. There is a market for solar panels, LEDs, super-efficient DC fans, chargers, and DC cooking appliances, all of which are now produced by Indian manufacturers.
3 Expand products and services to existing wholesale customers *and* start exporting to other Walmart locations globally.
 – Do all of robust action #2.
 – Export produce from the farming cooperatives.
 – Export "consumer durables" – solar panels, LEDs, super-efficient DC fans, chargers, DC cooking appliances, etc.
 – Export free-standing solar power and lighting systems.

4 Accept the government's demand to obtain 30 percent of supply
   from local sources, start the limited retail operations that are per-
   mitted, and expand sourcing from India for global operations.
   – Develop farm cooperatives for producing organic and high-
     quality produce.
   – Build the retail stores to be independent of the unreliable
     AC power grid, by employing local, green DC power
     generation.
   – Add locally sourced, freestanding solar power and DC
     lighting and appliances to the product portfolio.[8]
   – Expand sourcing from India for global operations
       a Expand farming cooperatives rapidly, in collaboration
         with proven local partners,[9] and start exporting
         produce.
       b Introduce freestanding systems of solar power, and
         DC lighting and appliances to the product portfolio,
         for less developed economies, and for people in
         developed economies who wish to be more "green" or
         independent of the grid.

The inclusion of DC power sources and systems is driven by the
fact that a significant *change in Walmart's value chain* for its retail
stores is associated with its local, green and efficient power generation and lighting. A related technology is DC power, which, some
believe, will disrupt the widespread use of AC power.[10] Distributed
green power generation has been identified as a new competency
that Walmart possesses.

Robust Action #3 ("Expand products and services to existing
wholesale customers *and* start exporting to other Walmart locations globally") and Robust Action #4 ("Accept the government's
demand to obtain 30 percent of supply from local sources, start the
limited retail operations that are permitted, and expand sourcing
from India for global operations") are also intended to reposition

Walmart to shift the perceptions of the Indian government, which is a key and currently somewhat adversarial stakeholder, into a supportive frame of mind. Figure 10.2 redoes the stakeholder classification matrix from chapter 3, with special application to Walmart.

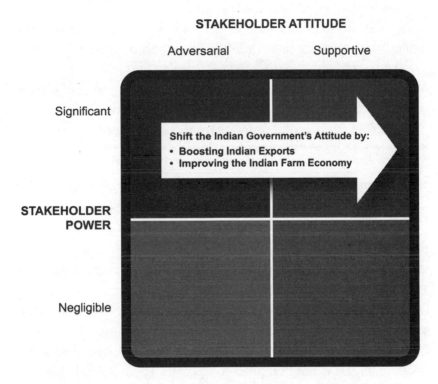

STAKEHOLDER ATTITUDE

Adversarial   Supportive

Significant

Shift the Indian Government's Attitude by:
• Boosting Indian Exports
• Improving the Indian Farm Economy

STAKEHOLDER POWER

Negligible

Figure 10.2 Stakeholder Classification Matrix Applied to Walmart in India

Applying the Multi-Criteria Decision Model to Walmart's Robust Actions

Continuing to employ Expert Choice software, the robust actions and related strategies were assessed using the criteria and weights described earlier. The resulting weight for each of the four robust actions is as follows:

1 Continue existing cash-and-carry wholesale warehouses.
   (Attractiveness: 15.4 on a 100-point scale.)
2 Expand products and services to existing wholesale customers.
   (Attractiveness: 27.9 on a 100-point scale.)
3 Expand products and services to existing wholesale customers *and* start exporting to other Walmart locations globally.
   (Attractiveness: 61.6 on a 100-point scale.)
4 Accept the government's demand to obtain 30 percent of supply from local sources, start the limited retail operations that are permitted, and expand sourcing from India for global operations.
   (Attractiveness: 71.6 on a 100-point scale.)

The highest-rated strategy, surprisingly, is "Accept the government's demand to obtain 30 percent of supply from local sources, start the limited retail operations that are permitted, and expand sourcing from India for global operations." On closer inspection, however, this strategy is compatible with the wholesale cash-and-carry business. The retail strategy could focus on the growing urban middle class (which consists today of about 300 million people), while the wholesale strategy could be oriented to the rural population, which is over 700 million people, and to the urban population in the Indian states, where Walmart is not permitted to operate. The wholesale business is attractive on its own and could support the development of local sources of supply. It is not constrained by restrictive regulations and could generate profits and growth that would sustain Walmart's presence in India while the retail strategy is being developed.

A Modular Structure for Walmart

To implement this Wicked Strategy, Walmart would need to implement a modular structure. The existing wholesale business is an established operation that is appropriately managed as a cluster unit, an SBU. The retail operation would be a startup, a collateral unit. This collateral unit would have to shoulder the challenging task of meeting the onerous demands made by the government in a fashion that motivates the government to permit rapid expansion beyond the initially approved retail locations.

Both the cluster unit and the collateral unit would report to an Indian headquarters, a core unit. The recommended retail strategy and the compatible, wholesale strategy, implemented by the collateral unit and the cluster unit respectively, need to be coordinated by the core unit because they utilize common products, resources, and competencies. For instance, the farming cooperatives and the DC power products relate to both strategies. The money transfer service that employs wholesalers and cell phones may be of interest to urban dwellers (those targeted by the retail strategy), who need to send money to rural relatives (those targeted by the wholesale strategy).

Organizationally, a single point of contact with the government, perhaps the most important stakeholder, would be desirable. But the separation of the markets still needs to be maintained. The urban middle class and the rural poor have different needs that must be separately addressed by the products and services offered. Moreover, the retail strategy is experimental and needs to be managed differently than the more established wholesale strategy. So, with the cluster and collateral units addressing the wholesale and retail strategies respectively, the core unit would focus on government relations and the development of indigenous supply chains, concentrating on farm produce and DC power.

It is interesting to note that Walmart's corporate headquarters currently does work on the development of competencies. It works on creating and strengthening competencies like RFID in partnership with the University of Arkansas in Bentonville. Its logistics and supply chain expertise has its roots and continuing development in the headquarters. Similar development of locally needed competencies is what is expected of the Indian core unit in the context of the modular structure.

If performance falls short and desired growth is not achieved, the entire India organization could be sold, or just the collateral unit could be terminated or sold. If, in due course, the restrictions on the number and location of retail stores in India are lifted, Walmart could then invest massively in what promises to become the largest retail market in the world. This is the *real options* approach in play, with a truly enormous upside.

A Wicked Strategy for Walmart

The recommended strategy possesses characteristics that entitle it to be called a "Wicked Strategy." It reverses the conclusion of the classic strategy analysis, implemented by Walmart, which is to withdraw from the retail business in India, because the current business model has limited growth potential, a key stakeholder is adversarial, and the future is uncertain and complex. This conclusion may appear logical, but is an admission of defeat.

The Wicked Strategy emerges because Walmart:

1 Recognizes the pull of *globalization* and the attraction of a country with the second-largest population (soon to be the largest) in the world, a growing economy, and a rapidly expanding middle class.
2 *Innovates* by embracing a *disruptive technology* (the shift to DC power) to open up new lines of business.
3 *Co-creates value* with Indian farmers, and with Indian companies investing in DC technology, developing their capabilities and their earning potential.
4 *Shares value* with suppliers, opening new global markets for them.

5   Becomes *one with the customers*, both consumers and
     wholesalers, recognizing their unique needs like electricity,
     financial services, and business networking through technology.
6   Improves the *quality of life* for the Indian consumer, *fulfilling
     the company mission* and operationalizing, in the process, a
     fundamental *value* that the company embraces.
7   Uses a judo-like approach to *convert a constraint into an
     opportunity* by accepting the government mandate about local
     sources of supply and, by growing them and incorporating
     them in the global supply chain, taking advantage of their low-
     cost characteristics.
8   Expects that shifting the government's attitude, by responding
     positively to its mandate, may ease the regulatory constraints
     placed on Walmart in the retail business. As the government
     continues to observe the *societal benefits* that Walmart generates,
     it may be more inclined to welcome Walmart's greater
     participation in the Indian economy. And, even if the restraints
     are not lifted, there are profits to be made and growth to be
     gained by improving Walmart's low-cost sources of supply.
9   Adopts a *real options* approach that keeps Walmart in the
     game, with the possibility of making additional major
     investments in retail stores if regulations change.
10 Uses *feed-forward* to envision robust actions and new business
     models, and lay the foundation for a desired future.
11 Implements a *modular structure* that gives the Indian retail
     and wholesale strategies the freedom and motivation to build
     synergies and innovate, and that develops the indigenous
     supply chain *competencies* that are part of a new business
     model.
12 Employs its *identity* – *values* (quality of life and profits,
     responsible global citizenship), *aspirations* (growth and
     sustainability), and *competencies* (supply chain, logistics,
     DC power) – to identify the best strategy.

IN CONCLUSION

In a world of uncertainty and complexity – unsettled by the three mega-forces of globalization, innovation, and shared value, and directly challenged by disruptive technologies, conflicted stakeholders, and unknowable futures – wicked problems abound. Wicked Strategies that respond to wicked problems have to be built on the foundation of a culture that confidently embraces change and uncertainty as sources of competitive advantage and growth – growth in competencies, growth in benefits to stakeholders, growth in markets and people served, and growth in revenue and profits.

We now know some of the things that Wicked Strategies need to do in order to transmute chaos into cash flow. They need to specify breathtakingly ambitious goals; support an entrepreneurial, risk-taking culture in the firm; explore changes and disruptive possibilities along the entire value chain; embrace and generate disruptive technologies; plan from possible and visionary futures back to the robust actions and enablers that create a desired future; empathetically relate to the customer in order to develop new value propositions and business models; add dynamically and symbiotically to the array of capabilities that the firm possesses; and build a dynamic organization that is custom-designed to nurture new businesses and facilitate transformation while continuing to support existing businesses.

This may appear at first glance to be a daunting if not impossible task. But we know how to – and have seen real examples of how to – execute each of these steps to create and implement Wicked Strategies. It is my hope that formulating and implementing Wicked Strategies is a challenge that you are now prepared to accept and will confidently meet. What it takes is implementing the *feed-forward framework*, consisting of:

1 *Identity* that affirms and expresses *your*
   • Core *values*, emphasizing humane priorities and your relationship with key stakeholders

- Enduring *aspirations* that have a touch of hubris, a great deal of reach, and the character of BHAGs
- Distinctive array of *competencies*, understanding how they are interrelated.

2 *Feed-forward* that employs your *values*, your *aspirations*, and the firm's *competencies* as the criteria, appropriately weighted, for evaluating strategic alternatives, initiatives and new business models derived by

- Employing *possibility scenarios* to identify *robust actions* and *transformational scenarios* to identify *enablers* of a desired future
- Analyzing *value chains* to detect emerging disruptive *differences* in kind and identify competencies to be built, complementary resources and partners to be developed, and alliances to be established.
- Incorporating *social responsibility* into the business model

3 *Modular structure* that is designed to be dynamic and supportive of *feed-forward* by incorporating

- *Collateral units* for experimenting with entrepreneurial ventures
- *Cluster units* that serve as SBUs for supporting established businesses
- A *core unit* that serves as the firm's headquarters and is committed to developing and symbiotically adding competencies as its primary purpose.

What your efforts are designed to create is a firm that embraces change and transformation, yet maintains an enduring and proud identity; that prizes its employees as the creators of celebrated societal benefit and superior economic value for its shareholders; and that unflinchingly faces and indeed exploits an unknowable future.

Notes

Chapter 1: Wicked Problems and Wicked Strategies

1 Courtney, H., Kirkland, J., & Viguerie, P. (1997). Strategy under Uncertainty. *Harvard Business Review*, 75(6), 67–79.
2 Kumar, M. (2008). *Quantum: Einstein, Bohr and the Great Debate about the Nature of Reality*. Norton.
3 Wilson, D., & Purushothaman, R. (2003). Dreaming with BRICs: The Path to 2050 (Global Economics Paper no. 99). Goldman, Sachs & Company.
4 Friedman, M. (1970). The Social Responsibility of Business Is to Increase Its Profits. *New York Times Magazine*, 13 September.
5 Porter, M.E., & Kramer, M.R. (2011). Creating Shared Value. *Harvard Business Review*, 89(1/2), 62–77.
6 Prahalad, C.K. (2004). *The Fortune at the Bottom of the Pyramid*. Wharton School Publishing.
7 Hart, S.L., & Christensen, C.M. (2002). The Great Leap: Driving Innovation from the Base of the Pyramid. *Sloan Management Review*, 44(1), 51–6.
8 Pfitzer, M., Bockstette, V., & Stamp, M. (2013). Innovating for Shared Value. *Harvard Business Review*, 91(9), 100–7.
9 Courtney, Kirkland, & Viguerie. Strategy under Uncertainty.
10 Camillus, J.C. (2008). Strategy as a Wicked Problem. *Harvard Business Review*, 86(5), 98–106.
11 Zook, C., & Allen, J. (2003). Growth Outside the Core. *Harvard Business Review*, 81(12), 66–75.
12 Prahalad, C.K., & Hamel, G. (1990). The Core Competency of the Corporation. *Harvard Business Review*, 68(3), 79–91.

13 Strong, C. (2015). *Humanizing Big Data: Marketing at the Meeting of Data, Social Science & Customer Insight*. Kogan Page.
14 Radjou, N., Prabhu, J., & Ahuja, S. (2012). *Jugaad Innovation: Think Frugal, Be Flexible, Generate Breakthrough Growth*. Jossey-Bass.

Chapter 2: Disruptive Technologies

 1 Christensen, C.M., Raynor, M., & McDonald, R. (2015). What Is Disruptive Innovation? *Harvard Business Review*, 93(12), 44–53.
 2 Doz, Y., Wilson, K., Veldhoen, S., Goldbrunner, T., & Altman, G. (2006). *Innovation: Is Global the Way Forward?* INSEAD, Fontainebleau.
 3 Hart, S.L., & Christensen, C.M. (2002). The Great Leap: Driving Innovation from the Base of the Pyramid. *Sloan Management Review*, 44(1), 51–6.
 4 Hammond, A.L., Kramer, W.J., Katz, R.S., Tran, J.T., & Walker, C. (2007). *The Next 4 Billion: Market Size and Business Strategy at the Base of the Pyramid*. World Resources Institute International Finance Corporation, p. 3.
 5 Prahalad. *Fortune at the Bottom of the Pyramid*, p. 21.
 6 Christensen, C.M. (2013). *The Innovator's Dilemma: When New Technologies Cause Great Firms to Fail*. Harvard Business Review Press.
 7 See http://www.katz.pitt.edu/boh/case-studies/bttm-pyramid.php.
 8 Arvind's story is told by its chairman and CEO, Mr Sanjay Lalbhai in a video that is available at https://www.youtube.com/watch?v=VPC8Kn_XaSA.
 9 Immelt, J.R., Govindarajan, V., & Trimble, C. (2009). How GE is Disrupting Itself. *Harvard Business Review*, 87(10), 56–65.
10 Normann, R., & Ramirez, R. (1993). Designing Interactive Strategy. *Harvard Business Review*, 71(4), 65–77.
11 The term BHAGS was coined by J.C. Collins and J.L. Porras in their 1996 article "Building Your Company's Vision," in *Harvard Business Review*, 74(5), 65–77.
12 See http://www.katz.pitt.edu/boh/case-studies/vodafone.php.
13 Reverse innovation is the process of developing products and technologies in emerging economies and then taking them to the developed economies. It is the reverse of the traditional process of "glocalization," which is taking products from developed economies and modifying them for sale in emerging economies.
14 Brown, T. (2008). Design Thinking. *Harvard Business Review*, 86(6), 84–92.
15 Chen, H., Chiang, R.H.L., & Storey, V.C. (2012). Business Intelligence and Analytics: From Big Data to Big Impact. *MIS Quarterly*, 36(4), 1165–88.
16 Strong. *Humanizing Big Data*.
17 Kolko, J. (2015). Design Thinking Comes of Age. *Harvard Business Review*, 93(9), 66–71.

18 Eisenhardt, K.M., & Tabrizi, B.N. (1995). Accelerating Adaptive Processes: Product Innovation in the Global Computer Industry. *Administrative Science Quarterly*, 40(1), 84–110.

Chapter 3: Conflicted Stakeholders

1 Hamel, G. (2002). *Leading the Revolution: How to Thrive in Turbulent Times by Making Innovation a Way of Life*. Harvard Business School Press.
2 Bhalla, G. (2010). *Collaboration and Co-creation: New Platforms for Marketing and Innovation*. Springer.
3 Normann & Ramirez. Designing Interactive Strategy.
4 Pfitzer, Bockstette, & Stamp. Innovating for Shared Value.
5 The four freedoms identified by the FSF are: (1) the freedom to run the program, for any purpose; (2) the freedom to study how the program works, and change it; (3) the freedom to redistribute copies; and (4) the freedom to distribute copies of your modified versions to others.
6 Mehrpouya, H., Maxwell, D., & Zamora, D. (2013). Reflections on Co-creation: An Open Source Approach to Co-Creation. *Participations*, 10(2), 172–82.
7 Kanter, R.M. (1994). Collaborative Advantage: The Art of Alliances. *Harvard Business Review*, 72(4), 96–108.
8 Porter, M.E. (2011). *Competitive Advantage of Nations: Creating and Sustaining Superior Performance*. Simon and Schuster.

Chapter 4: Unknowable Futures

1 Herzberg, F.I. (1966). *Work and the Nature of Man*. Cleveland World Publishing.
2 Camillus, J.C. (1996). Reinventing Strategic Planning. *Strategy & Leadership*, 24(3), 6–12.
3 Gilmore, W.S., & Camillus, J.C. (1996). Do Your Planning Processes Meet the Reality Test? *Long Range Planning*, 29(6), 869–79.
4 Quinn, J.B. (1980). *Strategies for Change: Logical Incrementalism*. Irwin.
5 Lindblom, C.E. (1959). The Science of "Muddling Through." *Public Administration Review*, 19(2), 79–88.
6 Hayes, R.H. (1985). Strategic Planning – Forward in Reverse. *Harvard Business Review*, 63(6).
7 Fahey, L., & Randall, R.M. (Eds.). (1998). *Learning from the Future: Competitive Foresight Scenarios*. John Wiley & Sons.
8 Trigeorgis, L. (1996). *Real Options: Managerial Flexibility and Strategy in Resource Allocation*. MIT Press.

9   Camillus, J.C., & Datta, D.K. (1991). Managing Strategic Issues in a Turbulent Environment. *Long Range Planning*, 24(2), 67–74.
10 Eisenhardt & Tabrizi. Accelerating Adaptive Processes.
11 Brown. Design Thinking.
12 Veliyath, R. (1985). Feedforward Orientation in the Strategic Management Process: A Contingent Choice (Doctoral dissertation, University of Pittsburgh).

Chapter 6: Identity

1   Camillus, J.C. (2011). Organisational Identity and the Business Environment: The Strategic Connection. *International Journal of Business Environment*, 4(4), 306–14.
2   Williamson, O.E. (1979). Transaction-Cost Economics: The Governance of Contractual Relations. *Journal of Law and Economics*, 22(2), 233–61.
3   Grant, R.M. (2010). *Contemporary Strategy Analysis*. John Wiley & Sons.
4   Greiner, L.E. (1972). Evolution and Revolution as Organizations Grow. *Harvard Business Review*, 76(3), 55–60.
5   Weber, M. (1922, 1978). *Economy and Society: An Outline of Interpretive Sociology*. University of California Press.
6   APQC. (1999). *Turning Strategy into Action: Tools and Techniques for Implementing Strategic Plans*. APQC.
7   Mills, D.Q. (1991). *Rebirth of the Corporation*. Wiley.
8   Abell, D.F. (1980). *Defining the Business: The Starting Point of Strategic Planning*. Prentice-Hall.
9   Albert, S., & Whetten, D. (1985). Organisational Identity. *Research in Organisational Behavior*, 7, 263–95. Also see Camillus, Organisational Identity and the Business Environment.
10 Cyert, R.M., & March, J.G. (1963). A Behavioral Theory of the Firm. Wiley-Blackwell. Also see Camillus, Strategy as a Wicked Problem.
11 Prahalad & Hamel. The Core Competency of the Corporation.
12 Freeman, R.E., Harrison, J.S., & Wicks, A.C. (2007). *Managing for Stakeholders: Survival, Reputation and Success*. Yale University Press, p. 6.
13 Camillus. Organisational Identity, p. 308.
14 See, for instance, the foci of the "balanced scorecard" as discussed in Kaplan, R.S., & Norton, D.P. (1996). Using the Balanced Scorecard as a Strategic Management System. *Harvard Business Review*, 74(1), 75–85.
15 Simons, R. (2010). Stress-test Your Strategy: The Seven Questions to Ask. *Harvard Business Review*, 88(11), 93–100.
16 Nayar, V. (2010). *Employees First, Customers Second*. Harvard Business Press.
17 Pfeffer, J. (2010). Building Sustainable Organisations: The Human Factor. *Academy of Management Perspectives*, 24(1), 34–46.

18 Ibid.
19 Friedman. The Social Responsibility of Business.
20 Khurana, R. (2007). *From Higher Aims to Hired Hands: The Social Transformation of American Business Schools and the Unfulfilled Promise of Management as a Profession.* Princeton University Press.
21 Ibid., p. 3.
22 Camillus, J.C. (2014). The Business Case for Humanity in Strategic Decision Making. *Vilakshan,* 11(2), 141–58.
23 Cyert & March. A Behavioral Theory of the Firm.
24 Freeman, Harrison, & Wicks. *Managing for Stakeholders.*
25 Khurana. *From Higher Aims to Hired Hands.*
26 Kaplan & Norton. Using the Balanced Scorecard.
27 Barney, J. (1991). Firm Resources and Sustained Competitive Advantage. *Journal of Management,* 17(1), 99–120.
28 Ghemawat, P. (1986). Sustainable Advantage. *Harvard Business Review,* 64(5), 53–8.
29 Stalk, G., Evans, P., & Shulman, L.E. (1992). Competing on Capabilities: The New Rules of Corporate Strategy, *Harvard Business Review,* 70(2), 57–69.
30 Prahalad & Hamel. The Core Competency of the Corporation.
31 Chakravarthy, B., & Lorange, P. (2008). *Profit or Growth? Why You Don't Have to Choose.* Pearson Prentice Hall.
32 Teece, D.J., Pisano, G., & Shuen, A. (1997). Dynamic Capabilities and Strategic Management. *Strategic Management Journal,* 18(7), 509–33.

Chapter 7: Feed-Forward

1 Veliyath. Feedforward Orientation in the Strategic Management Process.
2 Camillus, J. (2015). Feed-Forward Systems: Managing a Future Filled with Wicked Problems. *Rotman Magazine,* Winter 2015, 52–9.
3 Dong-Gil Ko, D., & Camillus, J.C. (2001). Managing the Future: Planning Paradigms and Scenario Development. *General Management Review,* 3(1), 21–31.
4 Courtney, Kirkland, & Viguerie. Strategy under Uncertainty.
5 Fahey, L., & Randall, R.M. (Eds.). (1998). *Learning from the Future: Competitive Foresight Scenarios.* John Wiley & Sons.
6 Cappelli, P. (2015). Why We Love to Hate HR ... and What HR Can Do about It. *Harvard Business Review,* 93(7/8), 54–61.
7 Charan, R., Barton, D., & Carey, D. (2015). People before Strategy: A New Role for the CHRO. *Harvard Business Review,* 93(7/8), 62–71.
8 Boudreau, J., & Rice, S. (2015). Bright Shiny Objects and the Future of HR. *Harvard Business Review,* 93(7/8), 72–8.

9   Brandenburger, A.M., & Nalebuff, B.J. (2011). *Co-opetition*. Random House LLC.
10 Lindblom. The Science of "Muddling Through."
11 Krasilovsky, M.W., & Shemel, S. (1995). *This Business of Music*. 7th ed. Billboard Books.

Chapter 8: Modular Structure

1   Greiner. Evolution and Revolution as Organizations Grow.
2   Dumaine, B., & Gustke, C.A. (1990). "Who Needs a Boss?" *Fortune International*, 7 May, 52–60.
3   Lawrence, P.R., & Lorsch, J.W. (1967). *Organization and Environment: Managing Differentiation and Integration*. Division of Research, Graduate School of Business Administration, Harvard University.
4   Mills. *Rebirth of the Corporation*.
5   Tushman, M.L., & O'Reilly, C.A. 1996. Ambidextrous Organizations: Managing Evolutionary and Revolutionary Change. *California Management Review*, 38(4), 8–30.
6   Mills. *Rebirth of the Corporation*.
7   Charan, Barton, & Carey. People before Strategy.
8   Rowan, R. (1986). America's Most Wanted Managers. *Fortune*, 3 February, cover story.
9   Beall, D.R. (2008). *Formation, Evolution and Transformation of Rockwell*. Dartbrook Partners.
10 Pfeffer. Building Sustainable Organisations.
11 Pfeffer, J. (2010). Lay Off the Layoffs. *Newsweek*, 15 February 32–7.

Chapter 9: Forging Wicked Strategies

1   See Camillus. Reinventing Strategic Planning.

Chapter 10: Deploying Wicked Strategies

1   SWOT is a mainstay of traditional strategic analysis. However, it can only be applied in the context of an accepted strategy, because SWOTs can only be defined with reference to a specific strategy. At best, therefore, SWOT analyses can only tweak existing strategies. Developing a transformational strategy or business model is beyond the scope and capability of SWOT analysis.
2   See http://www.corporatereport.com/walmart/2014/grr/index.html.
3   See http://blog.walmart.com/five-ways-walmart-is-upping-its-sustainability-game.

4 See http://www.triplepundit.com/2012/11/walmart-shouldnt-pay-sustainability/.
5 See http://blog.walmart.com/five-ways-walmart-is-upping-its-sustainability-game.
6 See http://www.katz.pitt.edu/boh/prague.php.
7 A 100-watt DC system can, incredibly, actually support as many as three LED lights, two fans, and a cell phone charger. The Indian government is promoting distributed generation and the use of efficient DC power to compensate for the abysmally poor power situation with the national grid. See http://www.dw.de/new-technology-for-uninterrupted-power-supply-in-india-could-end-rolling-blackouts/a-17503462.
8 India is accelerating the development and use of DC power. The Low Voltage DC (LVDC) Forum of the IEEE is headquartered in Bangalore, India. It includes major corporations such as ABB, Crompton Greaves, GE, Larsen and Toubro, and Philips. Among its research and technical partners, the LVDC includes the Indian Institute of Technology, Madras, and the University of Pittsburgh's Joseph M. Katz Graduate School of Business and Swanson School of Engineering.
9 For instance, Walmart buys organic denim from Arvind, a long-established Indian company that has successfully created a major source of organic cotton by educating and partnering with marginal farmers, who farm on small, unirrigated plots In the process, the partnership has successfully stemmed the growing incidence of farmer suicides.
10 There is a ripple across the world, which is predicted to grow into a wave, with the development of DC rural micro-grids for villages at the bottom of the pyramid and, at the apex of the pyramid, locally generated DC power employed by computer data centers, which are the most sophisticated and significant consumers of electric power today.

Index

Page references followed by *fig* indicate a figure; page references followed by *t* indicate a table.